MONETARY, FISCAL AND TRADE POLICIES

INTERNATIONAL MONETARY FUND

ELEMENTS, REFORMS, AND ISSUES

MONETARY, FISCAL AND TRADE POLICIES

Additional books in this series can be found on Nova's website under the Series tab.

Additional E-books in this series can be found on Nova's website under the E-book tab.

GLOBAL ECONOMIC STUDIES

Additional books in this series can be found on Nova's website under the Series tab.

Additional E-books in this series can be found on Nova's website under the E-book tab.

MONETARY, FISCAL AND TRADE POLICIES

INTERNATIONAL MONETARY FUND

ELEMENTS, REFORMS, AND ISSUES

JUAN A. DUMAS
EDITOR

NOVINKA
New York

For permission to use material from this book please contact us:
Telephone 631-231-7269; Fax 631-231-8175
Web Site: http://www.novapublishers.com

Additional color graphics may be available in the e-book version of this book.

Library of Congress Cataloging-in-Publication Data

ISBN: 978-1-62808-288-3

Published by Nova Science Publishers, Inc. † New York

CONTENTS

PREFACE

The International Monetary Fund (IMF), conceived at the Bretton Woods conference in July 1944, is the multilateral organization focused on the international monetary system. Created in 1946 with 46 members, it has grown to include 188 countries. The IMF has six purposes that are outlined in Article I of the IMF Articles of Agreement: promoting international monetary cooperation; expanding the balanced growth of international trade; facilitating exchange rate stability; eliminating restrictions on the international flow of capital; ensuring confidence by making the general resources of the Fund temporarily available to members; and adjusting balance-of-payments imbalances in an orderly manner. This book evaluates the purpose, membership, financing, and focus of the IMF's activities and addresses key issues, both legislative and oversight-related; as well as reforms and economic condition in Egypt since the 2011 revolution.

Chapter 1 - The International Monetary Fund (IMF), conceived at the Bretton Woods conference in July 1944, is the multilateral organization focused on the international monetary system. Created in 1946 with 46 members, it has grown to include 188 countries. The IMF has six purposes that are outlined in Article I of the IMF Articles of Agreement: promoting international monetary cooperation; expanding the balanced growth of international trade; facilitating exchange rate stability; eliminating restrictions on the international flow of capital; ensuring confidence by making the general resources of the Fund temporarily available to members; and adjusting balance-of-payments imbalances in an orderly manner.

Congressional interest in IMF activities has increased since the onset of the financial crisis in 2008. IMF lending has surged in recent years, particularly in light of large recent loans to Greece, Ireland, and Portugal. In

2009, major economies agreed to substantially increase the IMF's resources and to move forward on several major reforms at the institution. These include increasing the voting share of emerging economies; revamping the IMF's lending toolkit to introduce greater flexibility and create new facilities for low-income countries; and creating a road map for resolving the fast-growing economic imbalances in the global economy between surplus and deficit countries. In late 2010, IMF members agreed to a doubling of IMF quotas, which would require congressional authorization and appropriations.

The United States was instrumental in creating the IMF and is its largest financial contributor, providing 17.72% of total IMF resources. Since voting shares are based on financial contributions, the large U.S. voting share provides the United States veto power over major decisions at the IMF. Both the IMF and its sister organization, the World Bank, are headquartered in Washington, DC.

At the Bretton Woods conference, the IMF was tasked with coordinating the system of fixed exchange rates to help the international economy recover from two world wars and the instability in the interwar period caused by competitive devaluations and protectionist trade policies. From 1946 until 1973, the IMF managed the "par value adjustable peg" system. The U.S. dollar was fixed to gold at $35 per ounce, and all other member countries' currencies were fixed to the dollar at different rates. This system of fixed rates ended in 1973 when the United States removed itself from the gold standard.

The IMF has evolved significantly as an institution since it was created. Floating exchange rates and more open capital markets in the 1990s created a new role for the IMF—the resolution of frequent and volatile international financial crises. The Asian financial crisis of 1997-1998 and subsequent crises in Russia and Latin America revealed many weaknesses of the world monetary system, which have only become more apparent in the wake of the 2008-2009 global financial crisis and the more recent sovereign debt crises in Europe.

This report evaluates the purpose, membership, financing, and focus of the IMF's activities. It also discusses the role of Congress in shaping U.S. policy at the IMF and concludes by addressing key issues, both legislative and oversight-related, that Congress may wish to consider, including

- the role of the IMF as a lender of last resort;
- the adequacy of IMF resources; and
- the effectiveness of IMF surveillance.

Chapter 2 - In December 2010, the Board of Governors of the International Monetary Fund (IMF, the Fund), the institution's highest governing body, agreed to a reform package that addresses two major concerns about the institution: (1) that the size of the IMF's resources has not kept pace with increased economic activity in the global economy; and (2) that the representation of emerging and developing economies at the IMF does not reflect their growing importance in the global economy. Key parts of the reform package cannot go into effect until a number of IMF countries formally approve the reforms. If enacted, these reforms would increase the size of the IMF's core source of funding (IMF "quota"), and increase the representation of emerging market and developing countries at the IMF to reflect more accurately their weight in the global economy.

Implementing the Reform Package, and the Role of Congress

IMF rules do not require formal approval of the reform package by all IMF member countries, but the support of the United States, as the largest shareholder at the institution, is necessary. Although many other IMF member countries have submitted their formal approvals for these reforms, to date, the United States has not formally approved these reforms. Under U.S. law, the Administration cannot do so without specific congressional authorization. Appropriations could also be necessary. Although some speculated that the Administration would submit a request to Congress for authorizing the reforms in 2012, no request was made. Some speculate that the request could come in 2013 and could be considered in the 113th Congress.

Implications of the Reform Package

Arguments for Reforms: Proponents argue that the reform package is necessary for maintaining the effectiveness and legitimacy of the IMF as the central institution for international macroeconomic stability. The IMF's core source of funding needs to be increased, they argue, in order to give the IMF the resources that it needs to respond effectively to financial crises. They also argue that the under-representation of emerging economies at the IMF is broadly perceived as unfair and reduces the support of several member countries for IMF programs and initiatives.

Arguments against Reforms: Opponents argue that since the IMF has found other ways to supplement its resources during economic crises, the IMF's core funding source does not need to be increased. Opponents are also skeptical that emerging economies support the existing norms and values of international financial institutions, and that these countries may prefer financial and trade strategies that are less aligned with those of the United States.

Potential Impact on the United States: Implementing the reforms would not increase total U.S. financial commitments to the IMF and would have little impact on U.S. representation at the IMF. The reforms would require transferring some U.S. financial commitments from a supplementary fund at the IMF (the "New Arrangements to Borrow," or NAB) to the IMF's core source of funding (quota). This transfer could require appropriations, depending on how the Congressional Budget Office (CBO) scores the transfer of funds. The share of U.S. voting power at the IMF would fall slightly, but the United States would still maintain its unique veto power over major policy decisions.

Chapter 3 - Congress, which annually oversees and appropriates $1.55 billion in bilateral foreign aid to Egypt, is following the political and economic situation in Egypt closely. Economic conditions in Egypt have deteriorated rapidly since the 2011 "revolution." Political uncertainty abruptly reduced foreign capital flows into Egypt; growth, while still positive, has slowed substantially; the central bank is at risk of running out of foreign exchange reserves; and unemployment has increased from 9.2% before the revolution to 12.3% in 2012.

Many policymakers and analysts fear that the fragile economic conditions in Egypt jeopardize the country's political transition and broader stability in the region.

Egyptian authorities and the International Monetary Fund (IMF) have been in negotiations for more than two years over an IMF loan to Egypt in exchange for policy reforms that, if successful, could stave off economic collapse and create more "inclusive" growth. The IMF reached tentative agreements with first the military-controlled Supreme Council of the Armed Forces (SCAF) in June 2011 and later with Egyptian President Mohammed Morsi in November 2012. The November 2012 program would have provided $4.8 billion in assistance, and other donors pledged about $9.7 billion in additional financing once the IMF program was in place. No agreement has been finalized or implemented to date.

Egyptian authorities have been reluctant to commit to economic reforms that may be politically unpopular and increase the country's debt. Pressure to cut fuel subsidies is a particular issue. More broadly, many Egyptians associate the IMF programs in the late 1980s and 1990s with adverse social outcomes. On its part, the IMF has resisted a program that does not have sufficient conditionality consistent with its lending policies. Continuing political concerns and uncertainty in Egypt have also contributed to the delay. In the absence of an IMF agreement, the Egyptian government has recently secured financial support from Libya and Qatar.

Issues for Congress

Some lawmakers who oppose ongoing U.S. bilateral assistance to Egypt may oppose any existing or future IMF support of Egypt, on several potential grounds. Some may be concerned that in the rush to stabilize Egypt, the Administration could be too lenient in terms of the reforms it seeks from the Egyptian government. Others may not want the Administration to overly politicize an IMF loan. They fear that the application of too much pressure on the Morsi government could make accepting a possibly unpopular IMF deal too politically controversial to pursue and that the lack of IMF involvement in Egypt could undermine U.S. interests in the region.

The United States makes the single largest financial commitment to the IMF, and, with the largest voting power at the IMF, the United States wields a high degree of influence over IMF decisions. If Congress wanted to shape U.S. policy toward Egypt at the IMF, it could pass a "legislative mandate" legislation directing the U.S. representative at the IMF to use its "voice and vote" to push for certain policies toward Egypt at the IMF.

Lawmakers may also want to use the terms of IMF conditions as "benchmarks" for the provision of existing or new bilateral economic aid to Egypt.

Congressional concerns about bilateral debt relief are, in part, related to the absence of an IMF agreement. Additionally, legislative language (S.Amdt. 44) proposed in March 2013, but not adopted, would have tied U.S. bilateral economic assistance to Egypt to, among other things, an IMF program.

In: International Monetary Fund
Editor: Juan A. Dumas

ISBN: 978-1-62808-288-3

Chapter 1

INTERNATIONAL MONETARY FUND: BACKGROUND AND ISSUES FOR CONGRESS*

Martin A. Weiss

SUMMARY

The International Monetary Fund (IMF), conceived at the Bretton Woods conference in July 1944, is the multilateral organization focused on the international monetary system. Created in 1946 with 46 members, it has grown to include 188 countries. The IMF has six purposes that are outlined in Article I of the IMF Articles of Agreement: promoting international monetary cooperation; expanding the balanced growth of international trade; facilitating exchange rate stability; eliminating restrictions on the international flow of capital; ensuring confidence by making the general resources of the Fund temporarily available to members; and adjusting balance-of-payments imbalances in an orderly manner.

Congressional interest in IMF activities has increased since the onset of the financial crisis in 2008. IMF lending has surged in recent years, particularly in light of large recent loans to Greece, Ireland, and Portugal. In 2009, major economies agreed to substantially increase the IMF's resources and to move forward on several major reforms at the institution. These include increasing the voting share of emerging economies;

* This is an edited, reformatted and augmented version of a Congressional Research Service publication, CRS Report for Congress R42019, prepared for Members and Committees of Congress, from www.crs.gov, dated March 21, 2013.

revamping the IMF's lending toolkit to introduce greater flexibility and create new facilities for low-income countries; and creating a road map for resolving the fast-growing economic imbalances in the global economy between surplus and deficit countries. In late 2010, IMF members agreed to a doubling of IMF quotas, which would require congressional authorization and appropriations.

The United States was instrumental in creating the IMF and is its largest financial contributor, providing 17.72% of total IMF resources. Since voting shares are based on financial contributions, the large U.S. voting share provides the United States veto power over major decisions at the IMF. Both the IMF and its sister organization, the World Bank, are headquartered in Washington, DC.

At the Bretton Woods conference, the IMF was tasked with coordinating the system of fixed exchange rates to help the international economy recover from two world wars and the instability in the interwar period caused by competitive devaluations and protectionist trade policies. From 1946 until 1973, the IMF managed the "par value adjustable peg" system. The U.S. dollar was fixed to gold at $35 per ounce, and all other member countries' currencies were fixed to the dollar at different rates. This system of fixed rates ended in 1973 when the United States removed itself from the gold standard.

The IMF has evolved significantly as an institution since it was created. Floating exchange rates and more open capital markets in the 1990s created a new role for the IMF—the resolution of frequent and volatile international financial crises. The Asian financial crisis of 1997-1998 and subsequent crises in Russia and Latin America revealed many weaknesses of the world monetary system, which have only become more apparent in the wake of the 2008-2009 global financial crisis and the more recent sovereign debt crises in Europe.

This report evaluates the purpose, membership, financing, and focus of the IMF's activities. It also discusses the role of Congress in shaping U.S. policy at the IMF and concludes by addressing key issues, both legislative and oversight-related, that Congress may wish to consider, including

- the role of the IMF as a lender of last resort;
- the adequacy of IMF resources; and
- the effectiveness of IMF surveillance.

Introduction

This report provides background information and potential policy issues for Congress concerning the International Monetary Fund (IMF, the Fund), which is the central multilateral organization for international monetary cooperation. The United States is the largest financial contributor to the IMF. Congressional interest in IMF activities has increased since the onset of the financial crisis in 2008. IMF lending has surged in recent years, including large loans to Greece, Ireland, and Portugal. Potential policy issues for Congress include the role of the IMF as a lender of last resort, the adequacy of IMF resources, and the effectiveness of IMF surveillance of financial and monetary conditions in its member countries and of the world economy.

BACKGROUND

Origins

Prior to World War II, there was no negotiated international regime governing international monetary and trade relations. It was the shared view among the allied powers that many characteristics of the international financial system during the period between the first and second world wars, including competitive devaluations, unstable exchange rates, and protectionist trade policies, worsened the 1930s depression and accelerated the onset of the war. To address these concerns, representatives of the 44 allied nations gathered in Bretton Woods, NH, in July 1944 for the United Nations Monetary and Financial Conference. Their goal was ambitious and largely successful—to create a cooperative and institutional framework for the global economy that would facilitate international trade and balanced global economic stability and growth.

At the Bretton Woods conference, Articles of Agreement for the IMF and the International Bank for Reconstruction and Development (IBRD), later known as the World Bank, were drafted and adopted. They entered into force, formally creating the institutions, on December 27, 1945, following the adoption of implementing or authorizing legislation within member countries.[1] The Articles of Agreement of both institutions constitute an international treaty, imposing obligations on member states, which have changed over time.

In the eyes of its founders, the IMF's purpose and contribution to postwar macroeconomic stability were threefold: (1) facilitate trade by restricting certain foreign exchange controls; (2) create monetary stability by managing a fixed (but flexible) exchange rate system; and (3) provide short-term financing to member countries to correct temporary balance-of-payments problems.

The U.S. Senate agreed to the ratification (by the President) of the Fund and Bank Agreements in July 1945. U.S. participation in both organizations is authorized by the United States Bretton Woods Agreement Act, as amended (Bretton Woods Act).[2] Unique among the founding members,

the United States, in the Bretton Woods Act, requires specific congressional authorization to change the U.S. quota or "shares" in the Fund or for the United States to vote to amend the Articles of Agreement of the IMF or the World Bank. The U.S. Congress, thus, has veto power over major decisions at both institutions.

The Bretton Woods Monetary System

From 1946 to 1971, the main purpose of the IMF was regulatory, ensuring IMF members' compliance with a par value exchange rate system. This was a two-tiered currency regime using gold and the U.S. dollar. Each IMF member government could choose to define the value of its currency in terms of gold or the U.S. dollar, which the U.S. government agreed to support at a fixed gold value of one ounce of gold being equal to $35. Unlike in the classic gold standard period (1880-1914), monetary policy was not strictly restricted by a country's holdings of gold. Member countries were allowed to intervene in the currency market but were obligated to keep their exchange rates within a 1% band around their declared par value.

When currencies (other than the U.S. dollar) came under pressure from short-term "balance of payments" imbalances that normally arose through international trade and finance exchanges, countries would receive short-term financial support from the IMF. In cases where the currency "peg" was considered fundamentally misaligned, a country could devalue (or revalue) its currency. By providing monetary independence limited by the peg, the Bretton Woods monetary system combined exchange rate stability, the key benefit of the 19th century gold standard, with some of the virtues of floating exchange rates, principally independence to pursue domestic economic policies geared toward full employment.[3]

Balance-of-Payments Basics

The balance of payments is an accounting of a country's international transactions with individuals, businesses, and government agencies in that country and those in the rest of the world.

It represents the sum of purely financial transactions (capital account) and those arising from the export and import of goods and services (current account), and other unilateral transfers (such as gifts or remittances).

A country's current account should be equal to the sum of the capital account and any unilateral transfers. If a country spends more abroad on goods and services than it receives, it incurs a current account deficit. The shortfall, or deficit, can be financed by selling assets or borrowing, which involves a private capital inflow into the deficit country (a capital account surplus). If, however, private sources do not cover the current account deficit, then it must be financed by the government through the sale of foreign exchange (official reserves), which is referred to as a balance-of-payments deficit.

With flexible exchange rates, the deficit (or surplus) is corrected by a market-driven adjustment to the exchange rate—that is, it depreciates or appreciates based on demand. No purchase or sale of official reserves by the government is necessary to operate a floating exchange regime. Under a pegged exchange rate system, however, countries cannot alter exchange rate values and so use their foreign exchange reserves to finance the balance-ofpayments deficit, leaving the currency value intact. When a country does not have adequate foreign exchange reserves to finance its balance-of-payments deficit, it can petition the IMF for financial assistance.

The first major challenge to the postwar international monetary system came in the early 1960s. The postwar expansion in international trade and economic growth required an increase in international liquidity, that is, an increase in central bank holdings of the two major international reserve assets, gold and the U.S. dollar. With the economic recovery of Europe well advanced, the slow growth in gold supplies was hampering the growth of international reserve assets. As early as 1960, global foreign dollar holdings exceeded the value of U.S. gold holdings (at $35 an ounce). The system could continue to function as long as countries were willing to settle their balance of payments in U.S. dollars instead of gold.

The international community's response was to create a new international reserve currency, the Special Drawing Right (SDR). The SDR also serves as the IMF's unit of account. Initially defined as equivalent to 0.888671 grams of fine gold, the value of the SDR was switched to a basket of international currencies following the collapse of the Bretton Woods system of fixed parity exchange rates in 1973. The current basket includes the euro, the Japanese yen, the British pound sterling, and the U.S. dollar.

By 1970, a large and prolonged U.S. balance-of-payments deficit was mirrored by its counterpart, large balance-of-payments surpluses in the other major industrial countries. As a result, much of the 1960s was characterized by substantial currency instability, as liberalized capital flows brought about repeated currency crises in the supposedly "fixed" exchange rate Bretton Woods system. Amid declining confidence in the U.S. dollar, foreign central banks increasingly became reluctant holders of U.S. dollars and began exchanging their dollar reserves for U.S. gold holdings. After several years of instability, the Bretton Woods system of fixed exchange rates finally collapsed in March 1973 when the United States severed the link between the dollar and gold, allowing the value of its currency to be determined by market forces.

From 1973 to the Present

A major purpose of the IMF as originally conceived at Bretton Woods—to maintain fixed exchange rates—was, thus, at an end. Although the IMF had lost its motivating purpose, it adapted to the end of fixed exchange rates. In 1973, IMF members enacted a comprehensive rewrite of the IMF Articles. IMF members condoned the floating-rate exchange rate system that was already in place; officially ended the international monetary role of gold (although gold remains an international monetary asset); and, nominally, but unsuccessfully, made the SDR the world's "principal reserve asset." Henceforth, member countries were allowed to freely determine their currency's exchange rate, and use private capital flows to finance trade imbalances.

The IMF was also given two new mandates, which became the foundation of its role in the post-Bretton Woods international monetary system. The first was for the IMF to oversee the international monetary system to ensure its effective operation. The second was to oversee the compliance by member states with their new obligations to "collaborate with the Fund and other members to assure orderly exchange arrangements and to promote a stable system of exchange rates." Consequently, the IMF transformed itself from being an international monetary institution focused almost exclusively on issues of foreign exchange convertibility and stability to being a much broader international financial institution, assuming a broader array of responsibilities and engaging on a wide range of issues including financial and capital markets, financial regulation and reform, and sovereign debt resolution.

The IMF also increasingly relied on its lending powers, as floating exchange rates and the growth of international capital flows led to more frequent, and increasingly severe, financial crises. Over the past several decades, the IMF has been involved in the oil crisis of the 1970s; the Latin American debt crisis of the 1980s; the transition to market-oriented economies following the collapse of communism; currency crises in East Asia, South America, and Russia; and, most recently, the global response to the 2008-2009 global financial crisis and the 2010-2011 European sovereign debt crisis.

INSTITUTIONAL ASPECTS

Organizational Structure

The IMF Articles provide for a three-tiered governance structure with a Board of Governors, an Executive Board, and a Managing Director (*Figure 1*).

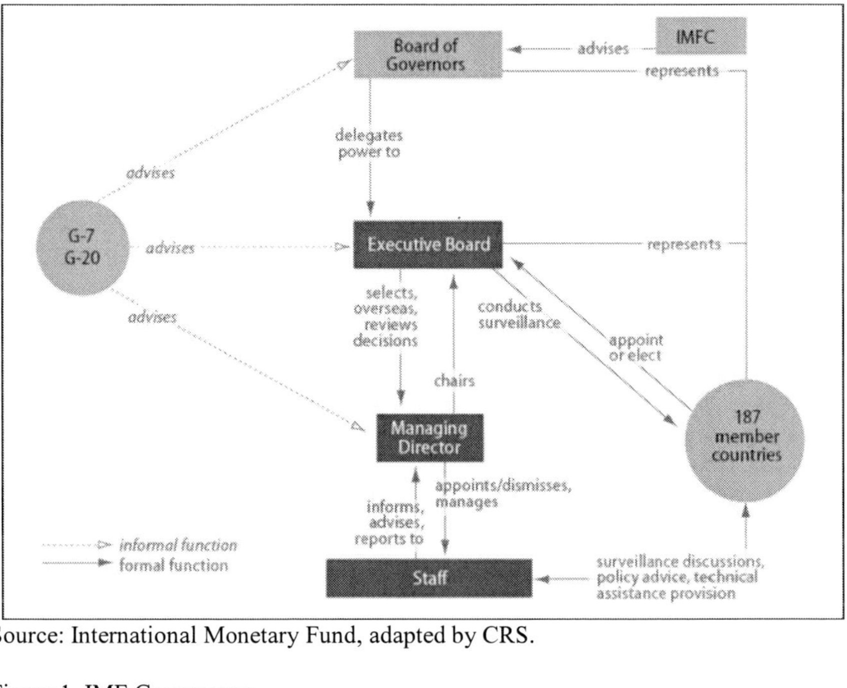

Source: International Monetary Fund, adapted by CRS.

Figure 1. IMF Governance.

The Board of Governors is the highest policy-making authority of the IMF. All countries are represented on the Board of Governors, usually at the finance minister or central bank governor level. IMF Governors usually meet annually at the fall IMF meetings. A committee of the Governors, the International Monetary and Financial Committee (IMFC), meets twice annually to consider major policy issues affecting the international monetary system and makes recommendations to the full Board of Governors. The Development Committee, a joint committee of the Boards of Governors of the IMF and World Bank, also meets at the same time to consider development policy issues and other matters affecting developing countries. The two committees generally issue communiqués at the close of their meetings, summarizing their findings and recommendations. These often serve as policy guidance to the IMF and the World Bank and as a means for airing views and for coordinating or harmonizing country policies on issues of international concern.

Day-to-day authority over operational policy, lending, and other matters is vested in the Board of Executive Directors, a 24-member body that meets three or more times a week to oversee and supervise the activities of the IMF. The five largest shareholders are entitled to appoint their own Executive Director.[4] The remaining members are elected by groups of countries, generally on the basis of geographical or historical affinity. A few countries—Saudi Arabia, China and Russia— have enough votes to elect their own Executive Directors. In reforms approved by the Governors in December 2010, the IMF Articles of Agreement will eventually be amended so that the Executive Board will consist solely of elected Directors, doing away with the practice of some member countries appointing their representatives.

The IMF Executive Board selects the Managing Director of the IMF, who serves as its chairman and chief executive officer. The Managing Director is elected for a five-year renewable term of office. The Executive Board also approves the selection of the Managing Director's principal assistants, the First Deputy Managing Director and three Deputy Managing Directors. The Managing Director manages the ongoing operations of the Fund (under the policy direction of the Executive Board); supervises some 2,800 staff members; and oversees the preparation of policy papers, loan proposals, and other documents that go before the Executive Board for its approval.

By tradition, the European countries nominate the IMF Managing Director.[5] The United States has a similar prerogative at the World Bank. The First Deputy Managing Director of the IMF is typically a U.S. citizen. Leadership selection has been a longstanding issue of concern. Emerging economic powers argue that any agreement that grants the leadership position based on nationality limits the pool of potential candidates. During the most recent transition from Dominique Strauss-Kahn to Christine Lagarde, however, non-European countries were unable to coalesce on a candidate, securing the position for a European.

Some analysts argue that calls for a non-European director from the emerging economies mask divides that make it difficult for emerging economies to unite behind one credible candidate. These calls, the argument goes, are part of the larger issue of the influence of emerging economies in the international financial institutions, and could ultimately lead to additional shifts toward emerging economies, despite Europe's hold on the top position. Evidence suggests that some shifts are underway. In July 2011, new Managing Director Lagarde elevated Zhu Min, a Chinese national serving as an advisor to the Managing Director, to Deputy Managing Director.

In addition to the official representation of the Board of Governors and the Executive Board, several other cross-cutting groups of countries are actively involved with the IMF. These include forums such as the Group of Seven (G-7) meeting of the finance ministers,[6] the Group of 20 major economies (G-20),[7] which in 2009 was declared by its members as the premier forum for international economic cooperation,[8] and the Intergovernmental Group of Twenty-Four on International Monetary Affairs and Development (G-24),[9] which coordinates the position of developing countries on monetary and development issues.

Quotas

Quotas are the primary national contribution to the IMF and are the foundation of country representation at the IMF. When a country joins the Fund, it is assigned a quota based on its relative weight in the global economy. Economic considerations include a member's GDP, openness to trade, volume of current account transactions, and level of official reserves.

A country's quota determines:

- *Subscriptions:* the amount of financial resources each member is required to contribute to the Fund;
- *Access to Financing:* the amount of financing a member may receive from the Fund; and
- *Voting Power:* the ability to formally influence the IMF's decisions.

The total of all member countries' quota subscriptions is 238 billion IMF Special Drawing Rights (SDRs), approximately \$376 billion.[10] Upon joining the Fund, a country normally pays up to one-quarter of its quota, the so-called "reserve tranche," in the form of reserve assets, widely accepted foreign currencies (such as the U.S. dollar, euro, yen, pound sterling), or special drawing rights (SDRs). The remaining three-quarters are paid in the country's own currency.

Supplemental Facilities

In addition to its regular quota resources, the IMF maintains two standing multilateral borrowing arrangements—the New Arrangements to Borrow (NAB) and the General Arrangements to Borrow (GAB). These are backstop resources intended to temporarily supplement available quota resources and borrowing. If activated, participating creditor countries make loans to the IMF, and the IMF uses those funds to provide loans to eligible countries.

The NAB is a set of credit arrangements between the IMF and a group of member countries and institutions, including advanced economies and a number of emerging market countries. The NAB is the facility of first and principal recourse in circumstances in which the IMF needs to supplement its quota resources. Once activated, it can provide supplementary resources of up to SDR 367.5 billion (about \$586 billion) to the IMF. The U.S. commitment to the NAB is \$100 billion.11 The IMF does not hold the NAB funds; rather, the IMF will call on NAB members to provide a percentage of funds that these members have committed if and when the Fund needs to use them. U.S. commitments to NAB are in the possession of the United States until the IMF requests that funds be released. If NAB members choose not to activate the NAB, the GAB, which was established in 1962, allows the IMF to borrow up to \$26 billion from 11 industrial countries.

Voting and Influence at the IMF

The Executive Board or Board of Governors of the IMF can approve loans, policy decisions, and many other matters by a simple majority vote. However, a supermajority vote is required to approve major IMF decisions. The supermajority may require a 70% or 85% vote, depending on the issue. A 70% majority is required to resolve financial and operational issues such as the interest rate on IMF loans or the interest rate on SDR holdings. An 85% majority is required for the most important decisions, such as the admission of new members, increases in quotas, allocations of SDRs, and amendments to the IMF's Articles of Agreement.

As *Figure 2* shows, voting at the IMF is highly concentrated, with 10 countries controlling over 50% of the voting shares (*Table 1*). With a voting share of 16.75%, the United States is the only country able to unilaterally veto major IMF decisions (i.e., those requiring an 85% majority). The United States also exercises a substantial amount of informal power at the IMF, given its large quota share and the location of the Fund in Washington, DC.[12] According to one analyst, "the IMF is an instrument of the G-7 countries. There is no example that comes easily to mind of a position taken by the IMF on any systematic issue without the tacit, if not explicit, support of the United States and the other G-7 countries."[13]

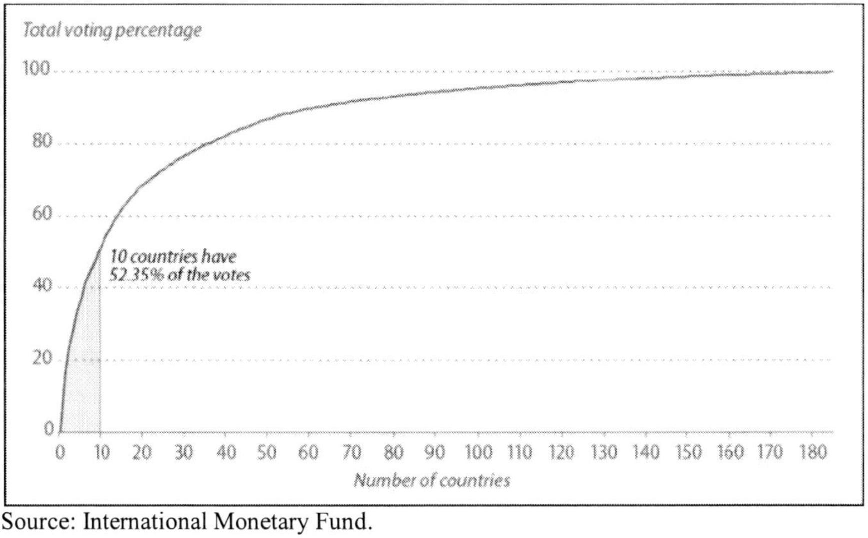

Source: International Monetary Fund.

Figure 2. Concentration of IMF Voting Shares.

The IMF states that its programs are based on purely economic factors, in order to seek an acceptable balance between protecting the interests of individual members and those of the membership as a whole. In practice, however, many analysts contend that the IMF is a highly politicized institution, reflecting the wide power differential between a few advanced economies and the remaining membership. For example, some analysts argue that recent IMF lending to European countries has been greater, and on more lenient terms, than lending provided to developing countries. "History suggests that if this were happening to a poor country or developing country, the rich countries would have voted against [the loan]," argues Arvind Virmani, the Indian Executive Director at the IMF, commenting about the possibility of fresh IMF support for Greece.[14]

On account of the heavily skewed nature of IMF voting, some analysts also argue that the developing countries with strong political ties to the IMF's largest shareholders get more favorable treatment by the IMF than other developing countries. For example, researchers have found evidence that countries are more likely to receive IMF loans if their voting at the United Nations General Assembly is similar to that of the United States and other advanced economies.[15] At the same time, countries may not seek loans for the IMF, because they are politically unwilling to meet the IMF's economic conditions.

Table 1. IMF Members with Largest Quota and Voting Shares (as of March 21, 2013)

Member	Quota share (percentage)	Voting share (percentage)
United States	17.69	16.75
Japan	6.56	6.23
Germany	6.12	5.81
France	4.51	4.29
United Kingdom	4.51	4.29
China	4.00	3.81
Italy	3.31	3.16
Saudi Arabia	2.93	2.80
Canada	2.67	2.56
Russia	2.50	2.39

Source: International Monetary Fund.

Functions of the IMF

In practice, the IMF's mandate of promoting international monetary stability translates into three main functions: (1) surveillance of financial and monetary conditions in its member countries and in the world economy; (2) financial assistance to help countries overcome major balance-ofpayments problems; and (3) technical assistance and advisory services to member countries.

Surveillance

The IMF provides surveillance of the international monetary system "in order to ensure its effective operation" and to "oversee the compliance of each member with its obligations" to the Fund.[16] In particular, "the Fund shall exercise firm surveillance over the exchange rate policies of member countries and shall adopt specific principles for the guidance of all members with respect to those policies."[17] The IMF's general surveillance recommendations are not binding or enforceable. The effectiveness of IMF surveillance is dependent on the peer pressure exercised by other IMF member countries, and increasingly the global financial sector, as most IMF analysis of global economic risks is made now public.

The IMF engages in both bilateral and multilateral surveillance. IMF members agree, as a condition of membership, that they will "collaborate with the Fund and other members to assure orderly exchange arrangements and to promote a stable system of exchange rates."[18] In particular, they agree to pursue economic and financial policies that will produce orderly economic growth with reasonable price stability, to avoid erratic disruptions in the international monetary system, not to manipulate their exchange rates in order to attain unfair competitive advantage or shift economic burdens to other countries, and to follow exchange rate policies compatible with these commitments.[19]

Countries are required to provide the IMF with information and to consult with the IMF upon its request. The IMF staff generally meets annually with each member country for "Article IV consultations" regarding the country's current fiscal and monetary policies, the state of its economy, its exchange rate situation, and other relevant concerns. The IMF's reports on its Article IV consultations with each country are presented to the IMF Executive Board, along with the staff's observations and recommendations about possible improvements in the country's economic policies and practices.

In pursuit of its multilateral surveillance function, the IMF publishes numerous reports each year on economic conditions and trends in the world economy. These include three semiannual publications: (1) the *World Economic Outlook*, which provides analysis of the state of the global economy; (2) the *Global Financial Stability Report*, which assesses global financial markets; and (3) the *Fiscal Monitor*, which surveys and analyzes the state of public finances in member countries.

Financial Assistance

Notwithstanding its macroeconomic surveillance, the IMF is perceived as an institution that primarily provides temporary financing to troubled economies. The IMF's financial structure can best be characterized as that of a credit union (see box). IMF member countries deposit hard currency and some of their own currency, from which they can draw the currencies of other countries if they face significant problems in managing their balance of payments.

As noted above, supplemental resources are available from the NAB or GAB if quota resources are insufficient.

Mechanics of IMF Financing

The IMF's financing mechanism is rooted in the credit facilities that existed between central banks prior to the IMF's creation. Central banks would borrow from each other with the borrower purchasing the currency of the lender, and paying for it by crediting the lender's account with the borrower in the borrower's currency. Thus, when borrowing from the IMF, a member purchases from the IMF the hard currency of another member in exchange for its own currency. Repayment is effected through a reversal of the original transaction. The member repays the loan by paying the IMF hard currency and repurchasing its own currency that the IMF had acquired.

For the IMF to be able to lend, it has available, through members' quota subscriptions and NAB commitments, a pool of hard currency and SDRs. A quarter of a member's quota payment is normally paid in usable assets (SDRs or currencies of other members acceptable to the IMF), and the balance is paid in the member's own currency. When members borrow from the IMF, the pool contains more of debtor members' currencies and less of SDRs or currencies of creditor members. The reverse takes place as members repay their borrowings from the IMF.

Operationally, the IMF decides quarterly, based on the expected pipeline of member borrowings and repayments, which currencies are to be used (and up to what amounts) to finance and repay its lending.

The amounts transferred and received by these members are managed to ensure that their creditor positions in the IMF remain broadly even in relation to their quota, which are reported by the IMF on a quarterly basis. The most recent report, covering transactions between August 1, 2010, and October 31, 2010, reported that the U.S. creditor position was 22.5% of total quota available to finance transactions.

The IMF is required by its Articles to ensure that countries' use of its resources will be temporary and that loans will be repaid. Failure of a borrowing country to repay the IMF reduces the availability of financing for all other IMF members. In order to ensure that it gets repaid, the IMF imposes conditionality on its loans. Conditionality is also intended to correct the borrower's current account deficit by bringing about macroeconomic stabilization and economic adjustment.

In the past, there have been debates about whether the austerity conditions that are often the core of IMF conditionality are productive in increasing economic growth. In 2000, one heavily cited paper found that participating in IMF programs lowers growth rates during the program, as would be expected. In addition, however, the study found that once countries leave the program, they grow faster than if they had remained, but not faster than they would have without participating in the IMF program in the first place.[20]

After heavy criticism of the conditions attached to IMF loans to East Asia in the late 1990s, the IMF revamped its conditionality guidelines in 2002. Additional reforms, including new IMF lending instruments based on economic prequalification (ex-ante conditionality) rather than traditional structural adjustment (ex-post conditionality) also address these concerns.[21]

IMF Loan Programs

The IMF has several loan programs. The Stand-By Arrangement (SBA), which provides the bulk of IMF assistance to middle-income countries, addresses short-term balance-of-payments problems and typically lasts one to two years. The Extended Fund Facility (EFF) addresses longer-term balance-of-payments problems requiring fundamental economic reforms and generally runs for three years or longer.

In 2009, following the financial crisis, the IMF created the Flexible Credit Line (FCL). The FCL provides a credit line to countries that have strong economic fundamentals and policies, and that the credit line can be drawn on without new conditionalities being imposed. Unlike the SBA and the EFF, the FCL relies on ex-ante conditionality. As of July 2011, Colombia, Mexico, and

Poland have accessed the FCL. In 2010, the IMF introduced the Precautionary Credit Line, now known as the Precautionary and Liquidity Line (PLL), for countries whose financial situations would make them ineligible for the FCL. A country can request a PLL for six months with a limit of five times its quota. The only PLL program approved to date was for Macedonia in January 2011, although many expected some Eurozone countries to request access to credit.

The IMF provides loans to its poorest member countries on concessional repayment terms. These aim to help countries overcome balance-of-payments problems, but their conditionality puts less emphasis on cutting spending and more on economic growth-enhancing reforms. There are three lending facilities for low-income countries:

- The Extended Credit Facility (ECF), which provides flexible medium-term support to low-income members that have protracted balance of payments problems.
- The Standby Credit Facility (SCF), which addresses short-term and precautionary balance of payments needs, similar to the Stand-By Arrangements in regular Fund lending.
- The Rapid Credit Facility (RCF), which provides rapid access at low levels with limited conditionality to meet urgent balance-of-payments needs.

In 2010, the Fund created the Post-Catastrophe Debt Relief (PCDR) Trust Fund to provide debt relief to low-income countries hit by catastrophic natural disasters. The first recipient of the trust was Haiti.

Finally, the Policy Support Instrument (PSI) supports low-income countries that do not want, or need, IMF lending, but seek IMF macroeconomic advice, and a "seal of approval" of their economic policies as a signal to international donors and financial markets. To date, seven countries have received support from the PSI: Cape Verde, Mozambique, Nigeria, Senegal, Uganda, Tanzania, and Rwanda.

Trends in IMF Lending

Prior to the onset of the 2008 economic crisis, many analysts argued that the IMF was on the brink of irrelevance, as booming capital flows and commodity prices allowed the remaining IMF creditors to repay their loans. With developing countries no longer needing IMF lending, and the advanced economies largely ignoring the IMF's surveillance, the Fund's future looked bleak. At the same time, IMF resources, especially when compared to global capital flows, had declined over the past few decades. Prior to the crisis, this raised little concern because demand for IMF resources was low. This view changed quickly in 2008, as the economic crisis worsened, and the IMF's loan portfolio expanded from below SDR 10 billion in 2007 to over to SDR 96.4 billion ($141.6 billion) in February 2013.[22]

Figure 3 illustrates the significant change in the composition of IMF lending since 1970. Advanced economies accounted for over 75% of the IMF credit in 1970, during the waning days of the fixed exchange rate regime. By 1990, their share of IMF credit had dropped to zero, before increasing in the late 1990s (loans to Korea and Russia), and then after the recent financial crisis. In 2010, due to several large European programs, IMF lending to advanced economies accounted for 17% of total lending. Loans to Latin America began rising in the 1970s, but did not increase sharply until the 1980s debt crises, peaking in 1990. Loans increased after 2000 because of three large programs (Argentina, Brazil, Uruguay), but have since declined, and are now at historically low levels, along with Asian economies.

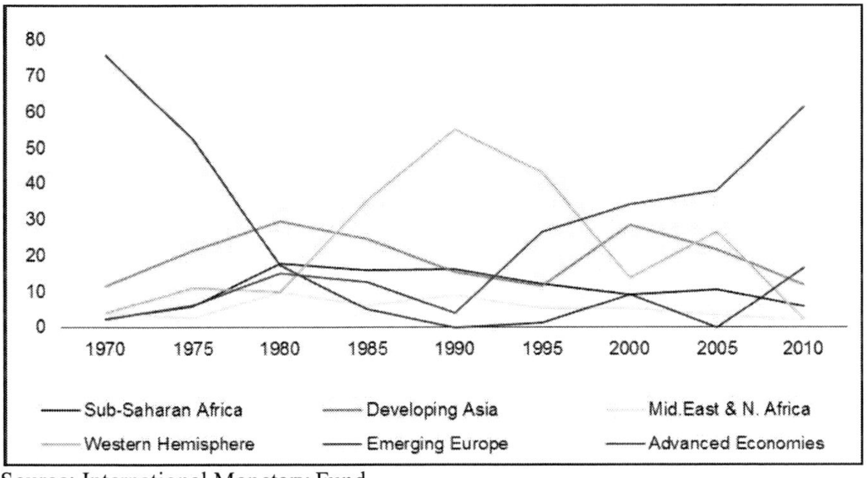

Source: International Monetary Fund.

Figure 3. Outstanding IMF Credit, 1970-2010. (percentage of total outstanding credit)

Another key trend is the increasing size of IMF loans compared to a country's quota. Officially, the amount a country is able to borrow from the IMF is related to the country's quota, its ownership and contribution share in the IMF. In most instances, countries may borrow several multiples of their quota in response to particular circumstances. The conditionality and performance standards attached to a loan become more rigorous and demanding as its size (relative to the borrower's quota) increases. In many cases, deemed exceptional by the IMF executive board at the time, countries have received much larger loans from the IMF than are allowed under normal guidelines. The 2010 loan to Greece, for example, was 3,212% of Greece's quota at the IMF. The 2011 loan to Ireland was 2,322% of its quota.

Technical Assistance

Access to technical assistance is one benefit of IMF membership, accounting for about 20% of the IMF's annual operating budget. The IMF provides technical assistance in its core areas of expertise: macroeconomic policy; tax and revenue policies; expenditure management; exchange rates; financial sector sustainability; and economic statistics. IMF technical assistance supports the development of the productive resources of member countries by helping them to effectively manage their economic policy and financial affairs. The IMF helps these countries to strengthen their capacity in both human and institutional resources, and to design appropriate macroeconomic, financial, and structural policies. About 90% of IMF technical assistance goes to low and lower-middle income countries.[23]

U.S. Engagement with the IMF

U.S. Policy-Making Process

As the largest single shareholder of IMF quota (approximately $67.35 billion), and contributor to the NAB ($100 billion), the United States has a leading role in shaping the IMF's lending, surveillance, and advisory operations. While the statutory framework for U.S. participation in the IMF provides the President the authority to appoint the U.S. Governor, Alternate Governor, Executive Director, and Alternate Executive Director, the Department of the Treasury has been delegated responsibility to direct U.S. representatives at the IMF and to take a range of actions with respect to the IMF, including making contributions to capital increases and implementing congressional mandates. Congress is responsible for authorizing and appropriating all U.S. financial commitments to the IMF. The Senate has advise and consent authority over all persons nominated to represent the United States at the IMF.

U.S. participation in the IMF is authorized by the Bretton Woods Agreements Act of 1945.[24] U.S. representatives at the Board of Governors and the Board of Executive Directors are appointed by the President, by and with the advice and consent of the Senate, to terms of five years and two years, respectively. They have the right to remain in office until a successor has been appointed.[25] The Secretary of the Treasury, as a matter of practice, is nominated to serve as the U.S. Governor at the IMF. The Chairman of the Federal Reserve customarily is nominated to serve as the U.S. Alternate Governor. As discussed above, the Board of Governors has delegated substantial authority to the IMF's Executive Board, which carries out the IMF's day-to-day operations. The U.S. Executive Director and Alternate U.S. Executive Director serve as representatives of the United States to the IMF and present the U.S. government's positions. Executive Directors at the IMF, including those of those of the United States, are employees of the IMF.[26]

When the United States joined the IMF, Congress made an interagency group of executive branch agencies, the National Advisory Council on International Monetary and Financial Problems (NAC), responsible for instructing the U.S. IMF representative, under the general direction of the President. Unless the President overrode their recommendations, policy was determined by a majority vote of agencies involved. The initial interagency procedure did not work well, and in 1965, Congress approved a reorganization act that abolished the NAC as a statutory committee and transferred all of its responsibilities and authority to the President, including the responsibility for instructing U.S. representatives at the IMF. In 1966, President Lyndon Johnson delegated the responsibility to direct U.S. representatives at the IMF to the Treasury Department, where it continues to reside today.[27] The President reconstituted the NAC by executive order, but it became solely a forum where other agencies could advise the Treasury Department about policy concerns regarding U.S. participation in the international financial institutions.[28] Unlike in a U.S. government department or agency, changes in the IMF's operations cannot be brought about simply by changing U.S. law. As a result, congressional proposals for policy changes in the IMF are formulated as directives to the Secretary of the Treasury to instruct the representative of the U.S. government in the IMF, the U.S. Executive Director, to promote the desired change. These have often been formulated as an instruction to use the "voice and vote" of the United States to achieve the desired goal. Consequently, the term "voice and vote" has become something of a generic or descriptive term for those amendments to U.S. law that seek to bring about specific changes within the IMF. Over the years, "voice and vote" amendments have increased. In the context of the current debate over IMF funding for advanced European economies, questions have arisen over the extent to which congressional policy, as embodied in the "voice and vote" amendments, has been carried out.

Voice and vote amendments can be organized in three broad categories: "policy," "directed vote," and "reporting." Policy mandates seek to foster or advocate certain policies at the IMF by directing the Treasury Department to instruct the U.S. Executive Director to use his or her "voice" and/or "vote" on behalf of the United States at the IMF Executive Board. For example, the U.S. Executive Director is directed to (1) encourage the IMF to adopt internationally recognized worker rights for borrowing countries; (2) encourage and promote the integration of women into the national economies of IMF member countries and into professional positions within the IMF organization; and (3) urge the IMF to encourage member countries to pursue macroeconomic stability while promoting environmental protection.

The second category, directed voting mandates, require that the U.S. Executive Director oppose an IMF loan when a country meets or does not meet certain criteria. In practice, U.S. opposition can take the form of abstaining from voting on, or voting against, the IMF loan under consideration. Examples include when a country has been determined by the President to violate religious freedom, provide support for acts of international terrorism, or engage in the proliferation of nuclear weapons. Reporting requirements, the third category, require Treasury to report to Congress on various issues related to U.S. participation in the IMF. Congress enacted legislation in 2010, for example, that requires the Treasury Department to report regularly to Congress about economic conditions in heavily indebted advanced economies receiving IMF assistance.[29] These reports are to discuss the debt status of the borrower country, economic conditions affecting its vulnerability and its ability to repay, and its debt management status.

Authorizing and Appropriating U.S. Contributions to the IMF

As discussed above, quota increases are paid to the IMF by transferring 25% of the increase in hard currency and the remainder in national currency, typically through a letter of credit. Both hard currency payments and payments to the IMF under the quota letter of credit result in a budget expenditure only if cash is actually transferred to the IMF. When a transfer is made, however, the United States gets an equal and offsetting receipt—an interest-bearing, liquid international monetary asset, specifically the increase in the U.S. reserve position in the Fund. Under current budgetary conventions, these offsetting transactions are treated as an exchange of assets. As a consequence, they do not result in net budget outlays, and they do not affect the net budgetary position (deficit or surplus) of the federal government. Looked at another way, any debt (liability) incurred through the sale of securities to make this expenditure is balanced by an asset—the U.S. reserve position in the Fund.

Nonetheless, Members of Congress have often provided authorization and appropriations to increase the U.S. quota, reflecting congressional concern about increasing U.S. foreign liabilities, and their impact on the federal budget. Budgetary treatment for the NAB is identical to that of IMF quota increases: an exchange of assets, having no net effect on the U.S. fiscal position. A drawing by the IMF under the NAB would not constitute a contribution to the IMF's capital and would not, therefore, increase the U.S. reserve position in the IMF. Rather, it would constitute an interest-bearing loan to the IMF. *Table 2* provides U.S. contributions since the IMF's creation, and their budgetary treatment. An *Appendix* provides additional information on the budgetary treatment of U.S. contributions to the IMF.

Table 2. Budgetary Treatment of U.S. Contributions to the IMF

Event	Date Effective	U.S. contribution (approximate billions of U.S. dollars)	Budgetary Treatment	Appropriation (Yes/No)
Founding Subscription	1945	$2.75	Outlay	No
Quota increase	1959	$1.375	Outlay	No
Establish General Agreements to Borrow (GAB)	1962	$2.00	None	Yes
Quota increase	1966	$1.035	25% outlay, remainder issued as line of credit, outlay on call only	Yes
Quota increase	1970	$1.54	No outlay, exchange of monetary assets	Yes
Quota increase	1978	$2.10	No outlay, exchange of monetary assets	No

Table 2. (Continued)

Event	Date Effective	U.S. contribution (approximate billions of U.S. dollars)	Budgetary Treatment	Appropriation (Yes/No)
Participate in	1978	$1.87	No outlay, exchange of monetary assets	No
Supplemental Finance Facility				
Quota increase	1980	$5.34	No outlay, exchange of monetary assets	Yes
Quota increase	1983	$5.58	No outlay, exchange of monetary assets	Yes
GAB increase	1983	$2.45	No outlay, exchange of monetary assets	Yes
Quota increase	1992	$11.92	No outlay, exchange of monetary assets	Yes
Quota increase	1998	$14.55	No outlay, exchange of monetary assets	Yes
Establish New	1998	$3.4	No outlay, exchange of monetary assets	Yes
Arrangements to Borrow (NAB)				
Ad hoc quota increase	2009	$8.00	Outlay, credit reform scoring adjusted for market risk	Yes
NAB increase	2009	$100.00	Outlay, credit reform scoring adjusted for market risk	Yes

Source: C. Randall Henning, U.S. Interests and the International Monetary Fund, Peterson Institute for International Economics, Policy Brief no. 09-12, Washington, DC, June 2009.

POLICY ISSUES FOR CONGRESS

Increased attention to the IMF since the financial crisis has revived long-standing debates about the institution's role in the global economy and the future of U.S. support for the institution. Some analysts argue that with the end of the pegged-exchange rate system, the IMF is no longer needed and it should be abolished.[30] Others say the IMF is still vital, but needs to be restructured and refocused.[31] Still others suggest that new functions should be added to the IMF and its role in the international monetary system should be expanded.[32]

Events since 2008 have shown that substantial risks remain in the global economy. Global imbalances, exchange rate misalignment, volatile capital flows and exchange rate movements, and the accumulation of large stockpiles of foreign exchange reserves have led many analysts to question the functioning of the international monetary system, and by extension, the future of the IMF.

Three issues that Congress may wish to consider are (1) should the IMF act as an international lender of last resort; (2) are the resources of the IMF adequate to complete this function; and (3) can IMF surveillance be made more effective?

Should the IMF Become the International Lender of Last Resort?

A central challenge for the global economy, according to some analysts, is the lack of an international lender of last resort that has access to sufficient finance to prevent a systemic global financial crisis.[33] Cross-border financial integration has brought many benefits, through trade and increased access to financing, but has also increased the risk of contagion, whereby a crisis may spread beyond its borders to other, seemingly stable economies. This is especially evident among advanced economies, where many analysts argue that the proliferation of credit in the financial system—among advanced economies, gross assets and liabilities are 500% of GDP—reflects significant economic distortions in the underlying economies. As the recent 2008 financial crisis illustrated, a single event, the bankruptcy of Lehman Brothers, can trigger a sharp contraction of global capital flows in such a highly connected global economy (*Figure 4*).

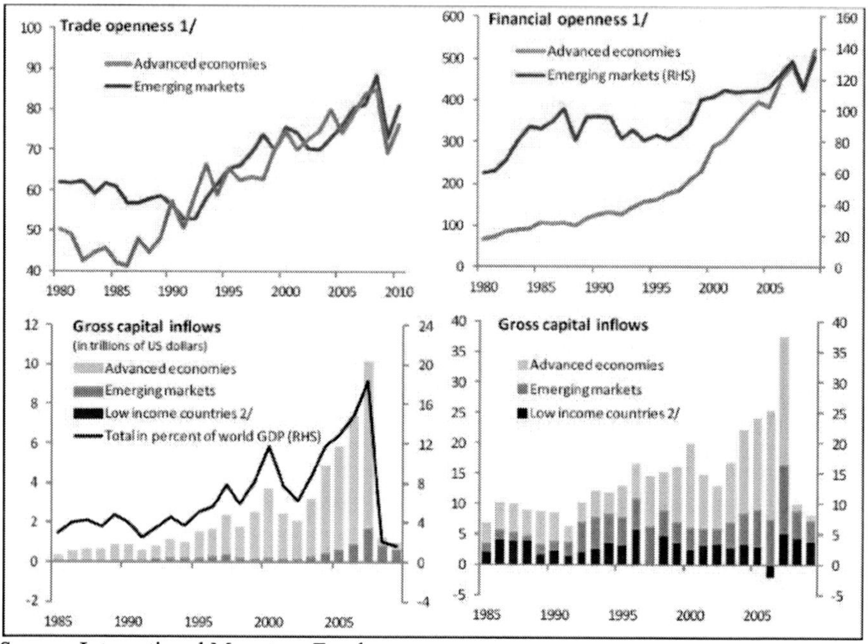

Source: International Monetary Fund.

Notes: (1) Trade openness is the sum of exports and imports as a share of GDP. Financial openness is the sum of external assets and liabilities as a share of GDP. (2) As classified in the IMF World Economic Outlook.

Figure 4. Increasing Global Linkages and Risks. (percent of GDP, unless otherwise indicated)

The challenge facing the international monetary system, and thus the IMF, is described by economist Maurice Obstfeld:

> In a world of integrated financial centers and multiple currencies, the boundaries within which a central bank can function as a last-resort lender no longer correspond to the boundaries within which a liquidity shortage *in its currency* can arise. Furthermore, the globally interdependent nature of modern financial relationships ensures that market turmoil *outside* the central bank's jurisdiction may well migrate *inside*. This is the basic problem.[34]

While many emerging and some advanced economies drew on IMF resources during the recent financial crisis, the majority resorted to an ad hoc network of central bank swap arrangements. At the height of the crisis, in the face of a massive global shortage of dollars, the U.S. Federal Reserve deployed over $600 billion in global liquidity to many other advanced and emerging economies, double the available resources of the IMF. The European Central Bank (ECB) set up €250 ($360) billion in swap lines, of which about €200 ($288) billion was with the U.S. Fed. In October 2008, the Fed also authorized swap lines of $30 billion each to four emerging economies with large exposure to U.S. financial institutions, Brazil, South Korea, Mexico, and Singapore. Thus, the Fed, and not the IMF, was the de facto lender of last resort for major economies. At the same time, several other countries, primarily in Asia, relied on their accumulation of foreign exchange reserves built up during the 2000s to prevent their economy from collapsing due to the liquidity crisis.

While central bank swap lines and self-insurance through reserve accumulation were effective in mitigating the effects of the crisis, and restoring liquidity in the global economy, the costs associated with these mechanisms are substantial, both for individual countries and for the system as a whole.[35] By their very nature, the Fed and ECB swap lines were selective, and subject to domestic monetary policy, as well as political pressure. It is uncertain whether the United States will be willing to play this role again in the future. Large accumulation of foreign exchange reserves is expensive, since they typically earn little interest and are susceptible to exchange rate risk. They also contribute to systemic instability, by creating excessive demand for reserve currencies, thus putting downward pressure on interest rates in the economies of reserve currencies, such as the U.S. dollar. Large swings in official portfolios of foreign exchange reserves can also have significant impact on exchange rates and the price of sovereign bonds.

Some analysts have proposed improving the Fund's lender of last resort function. For example, one recent study proposed three main elements of what such reform could look like: (1) an automatic trigger to access the facility; (2) unilateral country prequalification to the facility during Article IV consultations; and (3) liquidity funded by the world's "issuers of last resort."[36]

When considering expanding the role of the IMF, however, the concept of moral hazard has often been considered. As IMF lending increased after the financial crisis, especially after the large loans to Greece, Ireland, and Portugal, many observers, including some Members of Congress, raised concerns that financing by the IMF, particularly emergency financing provided during financial crises, encouraged the very behavior that it sought to prevent. Simply put, IMF lending may send the wrong signals to government officials. According to this view, in the best-case scenario, countries are spared the worst consequences of their poor economic decisions. In other cases, the IMF program may not stabilize the crisis, further indebting the crisis-afflicted country.

Other analysts argue that as the 1994-1995 Mexican crisis, the 1997-1999 Asian crisis, and the recent 2008 crisis have demonstrated, residents of IMF-recipient countries suffer painful consequences of a forced economic adjustment. The policy question is whether economic pain is mitigated by external financial support tied to a conditional economic adjustment program. A different type of “moral hazard” also arises with regard to investors. Does the existence of an emergency financial mechanism encourage private investors to take on risks that they might otherwise shun in an attempt to reap greater financial returns? In this context, some are troubled that, as a by-product of a “bailout,” professional investors, who took on higher risks and were probably rewarded with higher returns, are made whole.

IMF conditionality and pre-qualification of IMF loans might reduce concerns about moral hazard. Edwin Truman at the Peterson Institute for International Economics argues that the IMF’s role can be improved, addressing moral hazard at the same time, through a “comprehensive prequalification” process where the Fund presents “policy terms for lending” to every member country potentially eligible to borrow from the IMF, based on the IMF’s bilateral and multilateral economic surveillance.[37]

Adequacy of IMF Resources

To address the increased demand for IMF resources, world leaders at the spring 2009 G-20 meeting in London agreed to substantially boost the IMF’s lending capacity, primarily by a $500 billion increase in the size of the NAB. The Obama Administration proposed that the United States contribute up to $100 billion.[38] The requisite authorizations and appropriations were included in the FY2009 Spring Supplemental Appropriations for Overseas Contingency Operations (P.L. 111-32).

One of the reasons that world leaders increased IMF resources in 2009 via the NAB, and not through an increase in quotas, was long-standing frustration among emerging market economies that, after years of sustained economic growth, their representation at the IMF did not reflect their current economic position in the world economy.[39] Simply put, many emerging economies were unwilling to increase the IMF’s quota resources, unless there was also a shift in their share of IMF quota relative to the advanced economies that had traditionally dominated the institution. At the same time, a broad consensus has emerged that some European countries are over-represented at the IMF compared to their share of global GDP, especially in light of their representation on the Executive Board. European countries have three full seats on the IMF Executive Board, and currently chair or co-chair seven of the group constituencies.

At the April 2010 G-20 meetings, leaders pledged a shift of at least 5% of the IMF quota share to under-represented countries. On November 11-12, 2010, IMF member states agreed on a package of reforms, the core of which is a doubling of overall IMF quota to about $755 billion. In addition, there would be a significant shift of voting power to dynamic emerging market economies. If the reforms are implemented, the 10 largest members of the IMF will consist of the United States; Japan; the four largest European economies (France, Germany, Italy, and the United Kingdom); and Brazil, China, India, and Russia. The quota increase is expected to come via a repositioning of the NAB resources that were pledged in 2009. As part of the new quota increase to be completed by September 2012, member countries' commitments to the NAB are expected to be proportionally reduced to fund the increase in their quota.

Action by Congress will likely be required for the United States to participate in this plan.[40] According to one analyst, for the United States to participate in the quota increase, Congress would need to authorize a shift of about $65 billion from the funds appropriated for increased U.S. IMF participation in the FY2009 Supplemental Appropriations Act.[41] In addition to increasing the size and composition of IMF quota, there was also agreement on some reform of the IMF Executive Board, which would also need congressional approval since the IMF's Articles must be amended for them to take effect. These include

- the transfer of two European chairs to emerging market countries;
- the move to an all-elected Executive Board, eliminating the practice of appointing Executive Directors and allowing all countries to participate in Executive Director elections;[42] and
- establishment of a second alternate Executive Director position for multi-country constituencies with at least seven countries.[43]

Global Imbalances and IMF Surveillance

Since the introduction of floating exchange rates, there has been little pressure for major economies to address persistent global economic imbalances, which have increased sharply over the past 25 years. This holds equally for countries with large external surpluses, such as China and Germany, or those with large deficits, such as the United States and several European countries. Since the United States and Europe issue reserve currencies, their governments have over the past decade had greater flexibility to focus their economic policies on pursuing domestic goals, largely financed by greater amounts of foreign borrowing.

At their February 2011 meetings in Paris, G-20 authorities reached agreement on a set of three key indicators to assess the sustainability of national economic policies: (1) public debts and deficits; (2) private savings and debts; and (3) current account balances. While G-20 countries agreed on the indicators, there was no consensus on quantitative targets, reflecting deep-seated international disagreement over which countries, deficit or surplus, would bear the costs of reducing global imbalances. Thus, G-20 members only agreed to establish *indicative guidelines*— qualitative or quantitative benchmarks against which the indicators would be assessed—to determine the presence of large imbalances, and analyze the causes, implications, and corrective policies to address them. By request of G-20 members, the IMF is providing the technical analysis needed to evaluate how members' policies fit together—and whether, collectively, they can achieve the G-20's goals.

Although the current effort at multilateral surveillance is being driven by the G-20 countries themselves, many analysts remain skeptical that an agreement can be reached and enforced. The IMF has no disciplinary tools to enforce its surveillance. Any reforms that would provide such enforcement mechanisms would require amendments to the IMF's Articles, and in the U.S. case, the consent of Congress. As discussed above, currency values are determined in the marketplace, based partly on the strength of a country's foreign exchange reserves but mainly on the strength of its national economic policies and the market's confidence that sound policies will be maintained.

Some question, then, whether the new G-20 framework will be different than existing IMF surveillance. The IMF has the responsibility to monitor the international monetary system and the economic and financial policies of individual IMF member countries. In recent years, it has also monitored broader global and regional trends. Under its surveillance programs, the IMF can point to weaknesses in an economy but does not have any authority to enforce policy changes to address those weaknesses. Countries that do not need to borrow from the IMF have often shrugged off its advice. It is not clear under the current framework for the G-20 how the mutual assessments will translate into policy actions by participating countries on particular key issues, such as correcting global imbalances that may require increasing savings in the United States or increasing spending in China.

APPENDIX. U.S. CONTRIBUTIONS TO THE IMF AND THE FEDERAL BUDGET

When the United States joined the IMF, and for the first two quota increases, U.S. contributions were appropriated and recorded as an outlay on the federal budget. In 1967, the President's Commission on Budget Concepts recommended that U.S. transfers to the IMF be reflected on the federal budget as an exchange of monetary assets of equivalent value to the United States from the IMF, and therefore that they not be recorded in the federal budget as an outlay.

At the time of the next IMF quota increase, which became effective on October 30, 1970, the new budgetary concepts applicable to U.S. transactions with the IMF were not fully implemented. As a result, the transaction was treated as an exchange of assets rather than as a outlay in the official budget, as recommended by the President's Commission on Budget Concepts. For the next quota increase, which became effective in 1978, the U.S. share was subject to the budgetary treatment recommended by the commission: the quota increase was an exchange of monetary assets involving no budgetary outlay and requiring no appropriation.

At the time of congressional debate on the 1980 quota increase, Congress and the Administration agreed to incorporate appropriations legislation to reflect the fact that U.S. commitment to the IMF represented a line of credit. As such, Congress wanted control over the amount of contingent liability the United States undertook through its participation in the IMF. Since the United States received an equal asset at the IMF, and nobody could predict whether there would be any eventual outlays, a compromise was reached whereby U.S. contributions to the IMF (either quota or NAB) would score as budget authority (an act of appropriations would be required), but the contributions would continue to be scored as zero (i.e., no cost) on the federal budget, thus incurring no budget outlays (no effect on deficits/surplus).

In spring 2009, President Obama requested an increase in U.S. contributions to the IMF. When the request was transmitted to Congress, President Obama argued that treatment for U.S. contributions to the IMF should revert to the pre-1980 standard, and thus neither require budget authority nor incur any outlays. While many agreed with the Administration that it was unusual to record budget authority and not outlays, some Members of Congress raised concerns about not scoring any outlays for additional U.S. contributions to the IMF. They argued that such a method did not correctly reflect the degree of risk of the IMF defaulting on the U.S. contribution, given the current economic turmoil.

After several months of negotiation, on May 12, 2009, the White House and Congress reached an agreement to treat the U.S. subscription to the IMF as a line of credit for budgetary purposes. The Federal Credit Reform Act of 1990 provides that when the U.S. government makes a loan, it does not need to include the full face value of the loan in the federal budget. Rather, Congress must appropriate the estimated subsidy cost, an amount equal to the amount the U.S. government might lose from these loans as a consequence of defaults.[44] This procedure is used throughout the federal budgeting process. Unlike IMF quota increases since 1967, the U.S. contribution would be scored as a loan for budgetary purposes under the existing credit reform legislation with a commensurate budgetary impact. In the law authorizing U.S. participation in the new IMF funding plans, the FY2009 Spring Supplemental Appropriations for Overseas Contingency Operations, Congress subsequently appropriated $5 billion as a loan loss reserve to cover the risk associated with the new U.S. payments to the IMF.[45]

End Notes

[1] The third pillar of the postwar economic agenda, negotiation on multilateral rules to liberalize and govern international trade, was not completed until the 1947 General Agreement on Tariffs and Trade (GATT). In 1995, the GATT was succeeded by the World Trade Organization (WTO).

[2] P.L. 79-171, 22 U.S.C. 286 et. seq.

[3] Ibid.

[4] The five largest shareholders of the IMF are the United States, Japan, Germany, France, and the United Kingdom.

[5] For more information, see CRS Report R41828, International Monetary Fund: Selecting a Managing Director, by Martin A. Weiss.

[6] The members of the G-7 are Canada, France, Germany, Italy, Japan, the United Kingdom, and the United States.

[7] The members of the G-20 are Argentina, Australia, Brazil, Canada, China, France, Germany, India, Indonesia, Italy, Japan, Mexico, Russia, Saudi Arabia, South Africa, Korea, Turkey, the United Kingdom, the United States, and the European Union, which is represented at the leaders' level by the presidents of the European Union and the European Commission and at

the finance level by the rotating presidency of the European Council and the European Central Bank.

[8] CRS Report R40977, The G-20 and International Economic Cooperation: Background and Implications for Congress, by Rebecca M. Nelson.

[9] The members of the G-24 are Algeria, Argentina, Brazil, Colombia, Côte d'Ivoire, the Democratic Republic of Congo, Egypt, Ethiopia, Gabon, Ghana, Guatemala, India, Iran, Lebanon, Mexico, Nigeria, Pakistan, Peru, Philippines, South Africa, Sri Lanka, Syria, Trinidad and Tobago, and Venezuela.

[10] International Monetary Fund, "IMF Members' Quotas and Voting Power," and "IMF Board of Governors," available at http://www.imf.org/external/np/sec/memdir/members.aspx.

[11] To meet the U.S. $100 billion commitment to the expanded NAB, as well as an $8 billion increase in the U.S. quota at the IMF, Congress appropriated $5 billion in the FY2009 Spring Supplemental Appropriations for Overseas Contingency Operations (P.L. 111-32).

[12] Randall W. Stone, Controlling Institutions: International Organizations and the Global Economy (New York: Cambridge University Press, 2011).

[13] Lex Rieffel, Restructuring Sovereign Debt: The Case for Ad-Hoc Machinery (Brookings Institution Press, Washington, DC, 2003).

[14] Alan Beattie, "IMF Warned over fresh Greek Loan," Financial Times, July 8, 2011.

[15] Strom Thacker, "The High Politics of IMF Lending," World Politics, vol. 52 (1999), pp. 38-75. See also Axel Drehar, Jan-Egbert Sturm, and James Raymond Vreeland, "Global Horse Trading: IMF Loans for Votes in the United Nations Security Council," European Economic Review, vol. 53 (2009), pp. 742-757.

[16] Article IV, Section 3.

[17] Ibid.

[18] Article IV, Section 1.

[19] Ibid.

[20] Adam Przeworski and James Vreeland, "The effect of IMF programs on economic growth," Journal of Development Economics, vol. 62 (2000).

[21] Olivier Jeanne, Dealing with Volatile Capital Flows, Peterson Institute for International Economics, Working Paper PB10-180, Washington, DC, July 2010.

[22] For more information, see CRS Report RS22976, The Global Financial Crisis: The Role of the International Monetary Fund (IMF), by Martin A. Weiss.

[23] International Monetary Fund, Fact Sheet: IMF Lending, March 30, 2011.

[24] 22 U.S.C. 286 et seq.

[25] 22 U.S.C. 286a (a), (b).

[26] Federal law limits the salaries that IMF may pay the U.S. representatives, capping them at the rate of level IV of the Executive Schedule for the U.S. Executive Director and level V for the Alternate U.S. Executive Director.

[27] Executive Order 11269 of February 14, 1966, as amended, specifically delegates to the Secretary of the Treasury the President's authority to instruct representatives of the United States to the international financial organizations and to provide the U.S. government's consent with respect to IMF decisions. In addition, 22 U.S.C. 6593 specifically provides the Department of the Treasury with the primary responsibility to continue to coordinate "activities relating to United States participation in international financial institutions and relating to organization of multilateral efforts aimed at currency stabilization, currency convertibility, debt reduction, and comprehensive economic reform programs."

28 Since 1999, Congress has required that Treasury, as Chairman of the NAC, annually report to Congress on several topics related to U.S. participation in the international financial

institutions, including an assessment of the effectiveness of the major policies and operations of the international financial institutions; the major issues affecting United States participation; progress made and steps taken to achieve U.S. policy goals (including major policy goals embodied in current law).

[29] For more information, see CRS Report R41239, Frequently Asked Questions about IMF Involvement in the Eurozone Debt Crisis, coordinated by Rebecca M. Nelson, p. 22.

[30] Amar Bhide and Edmund Phelps, "More Harm Than Good: How the IMF's Business Model Sabotages Properly Functioning Capitalism," Newsweek, July 11, 2011.

[31] Edwin Truman, On What Terms is the IMF Worth Funding?, Peterson Institute for International Economics, WP 08- 11, Washington, DC, December 2008.

[32] Barry Eichengreen, Out-of-the-Box Thoughts on the International Financial System, International Monetary Fund, Working Paper no. 09-116, Washington, DC, May 2009.

[33] In a national economy, this function is typically provided by the central bank. See CRS Report RS21986, Federal Reserve: Lender of Last Resort Functions, by Marc Labonte.

[34] Maurice Obstfeld, Expanding Gross Asset Positions in the International Monetary System, remarks at the Federal Reserve Bank of Kansas City symposium on "Macroeconomic Challenges: The Decade Ahead," Jackson Hole, Wyoming, August 26-28, 2010.

[35] Maurice Obstfeld, Jay C. Shambaugh, and Alan M. Taylor, Financial Instability, Reserves, and Central Bank Swap Lines in the Panic of 2008, National Bureau of Economic Research, NBER Working Paper No. 14826, March 2009.

[36] Eduardo Fernandez-Arias and Eduardo Levy Yeyati, Global Financial Safety Nets: Where Do We Go from Here?, Inter-American Development Bank, IDB Working Paper 231, November 2010.

[37] Edwin Truman, The IMF as International Lender of Last Resort, Peterson Institute for International Economics, Real Time Economic Issues Watch, October 12, 2010.

[38] CRS Report R40578, The Global Financial Crisis: Increasing IMF Resources and the Role of Congress, by Jonathan E. Sanford and Martin A. Weiss.

[39] CRS Report RL33626, International Monetary Fund: Reforming Country Representation, by Martin A. Weiss.

[40] For more information, see CRS Report R42844, IMF Reforms: Issues for Congress, by Rebecca M. Nelson and Martin A. Weiss.

[41] Edwin Truman, IMF Governance Reform: A "Pretty Good" Step in the Right Direction, Peterson Institute for International Economics, November 8, 2010.

[42] Currently, members holding the five largest voting positions at the Fund appoint an Executive Director and are unable to participate in the elections that decide nominated Executive Directors.

[43] International Monetary Fund, "Factsheet: IMF Quotas," March 3, 2011.

[44] CRS Report RL30346, Federal Credit Reform: Implementation of the Changed Budgetary Treatment of Direct Loans and Loan Guarantees, by James M. Bickley (available upon request).

[45] CRS Report R40531, FY2009 Spring Supplemental Appropriations for Overseas Contingency Operations, coordinated by Stephen Daggett and Susan B. Epstein.

In: International Monetary Fund
Editor: Juan A. Dumas

ISBN: 978-1-62808-288-3

Chapter 2

IMF REFORMS: ISSUES FOR CONGRESS*

Rebecca M. Nelson and Martin A. Weiss

SUMMARY

In December 2010, the Board of Governors of the International Monetary Fund (IMF, the Fund), the institution's highest governing body, agreed to a reform package that addresses two major concerns about the institution: (1) that the size of the IMF's resources has not kept pace with increased economic activity in the global economy; and (2) that the representation of emerging and developing economies at the IMF does not reflect their growing importance in the global economy. Key parts of the reform package cannot go into effect until a number of IMF countries formally approve the reforms. If enacted, these reforms would increase the size of the IMF's core source of funding (IMF "quota"), and increase the representation of emerging market and developing countries at the IMF to reflect more accurately their weight in the global economy.

Implementing the Reform Package, and the Role of Congress

IMF rules do not require formal approval of the reform package by all IMF member countries, but the support of the United States, as the largest shareholder at the institution, is necessary. Although many other IMF member countries have submitted their formal approvals for these

* This is an edited, reformatted and augmented version of a Congressional Research Service publication, CRS Report for Congress R42844, from www.crs.gov, prepared for Members and Committees of Congress, dated February 1, 2013.

reforms, to date, the United States has not formally approved these reforms. Under U.S. law, the Administration cannot do so without specific congressional authorization. Appropriations could also be necessary. Although some speculated that the Administration would submit a request to Congress for authorizing the reforms in 2012, no request was made. Some speculate that the request could come in 2013 and could be considered in the 113th Congress.

Implications of the Reform Package

Arguments for Reforms: Proponents argue that the reform package is necessary for maintaining the effectiveness and legitimacy of the IMF as the central institution for international macroeconomic stability. The IMF's core source of funding needs to be increased, they argue, in order to give the IMF the resources that it needs to respond effectively to financial crises. They also argue that the under-representation of emerging economies at the IMF is broadly perceived as unfair and reduces the support of several member countries for IMF programs and initiatives.

Arguments against Reforms: Opponents argue that since the IMF has found other ways to supplement its resources during economic crises, the IMF's core funding source does not need to be increased. Opponents are also skeptical that emerging economies support the existing norms and values of international financial institutions, and that these countries may prefer financial and trade strategies that are less aligned with those of the United States.

Potential Impact on the United States: Implementing the reforms would not increase total U.S. financial commitments to the IMF and would have little impact on U.S. representation at the IMF. The reforms would require transferring some U.S. financial commitments from a supplementary fund at the IMF (the "New Arrangements to Borrow," or NAB) to the IMF's core source of funding (quota). This transfer could require appropriations, depending on how the Congressional Budget Office (CBO) scores the transfer of funds. The share of U.S. voting power at the IMF would fall slightly, but the United States would still maintain its unique veto power over major policy decisions.

INTRODUCTION

In December 2010, the Board of Governors of the International Monetary Fund (IMF, the Fund), the institution's highest governing body, agreed to a wide-ranging set of institutional reforms. If enacted, this reform package would increase the institution's core source of funding and expand the representation of dynamic emerging market and developing countries, such as Brazil, China, and Mexico, within the institution. In order for key parts of the reform package to take effect, IMF rules dictate that the reforms must be formally accepted by three-fifths of IMF members (113) representing 85% of the total voting power. Under this formula, although unanimous support is not required, approval by the United States, the IMF's largest stakeholder with 16.75% of the total voting power, is essential (see text box). To date, the United States has not formally approved these reforms.

Congress plays a pivotal role in determining the U.S. position on the current IMF reform agenda. Under U.S. law, specific congressional authorization is required for the United States to consent to change the U.S. quota, or "shares" in the Fund, which determine the United States' total voting power. Furthermore, depending on the budgetary treatment of any new authorized U.S. contributions to the IMF, appropriations are generally also required.

A majority of IMF member countries have approved these reforms, and with U.S. support, the IMF would meet the thresholds necessary for the reforms to become effective. News reports indicate that inaction by the United States on the reforms created tensions at the IMF-World Bank Annual Meetings in October 2012.[1] Some commentators have suggested that a lack of U.S. action may be frustrating for other IMF member countries, since the U.S. Administration was instrumental in advancing some of the reforms earlier in the process.[2]

This report provides information about the reforms, Congress's role in the reform process, and how the reforms could affect U.S. interests at the IMF. For additional background on the IMF.

Brief Overview: The IMF

With its near universal membership of 188 countries, the IMF is the central multilateral organization for promoting international macroeconomic stability. The IMF does this in three ways: (1) surveillance of financial and monetary conditions in its member countries and in the global economy; (2) financial assistance to help countries overcome major balance-of-payments problems; and (3) technical assistance and advisory services to member countries. The primary source of IMF lending resources is the financial contributions or quota subscriptions of its member nations.

When a country joins the IMF, it is assigned a quota based on its relative weight in the global economy. The distribution of quota is based on a formula currently incorporating several economic criteria: a member's GDP; openness to trade; volume of current account transactions; and level of official reserves. A country's quota determines the amount of financial resources each member is required to commit to the IMF. It also determines a country's voting power at the Fund and impacts the amount of financial assistance it may receive from the IMF.

There are two main decision-making bodies at the IMF. The Board of Governors is the highest authority in the IMF. All countries are represented on the Board of Governors, usually at the level of the Finance Minister or Central Bank governor. The Board of Governors meets annually at the fall IMF-World Bank meetings and takes major decisions on, for example, amendments to the IMF's founding document (the Articles of Agreements), quota increases and general reviews of quotas, and admittance of new members.

Although the Board of Governors has ultimate authority for running the IMF, it has delegated nearly all its powers to a resident Board of Executive Directors, which handles the operational daily activity of the Fund. The Board has 24 members each representing a single country or a group of countries, and usually meets three or more times a week to oversee and supervise the activities of the IMF, such as the approval of lending programs.

Unlike the United Nations General Assembly, which relies on a one-country, one-vote governance system, the IMF uses a weighted voting system based on a country's quota. The United States, with 16.75% of the total vote, has the largest single vote in the institution. The IMF uses a voting system in which the Executive Directors (EDs) can represent either a single country or several countries grouped in mixed-state constituencies. This constituency system produces a significant power asymmetry among members on the Board. Of the 24 Board members, the five countries with the largest quotas (currently the United States, Japan, Germany, the UK, and France) appoint their own executive director. The remaining 16 Executive Directors are elected. Some IMF members, including China, Russia, and Saudi Arabia, have enough votes to elect their own Executive Directors. The other Executive Directors are elected by groups of countries (or "constituencies").

Constituencies are flexible in their membership, and countries have periodically switched constituencies, often to a new group that will allow them to have a bigger vote or leadership role.

The IMF's Articles of Agreement set the various thresholds required for IMF decisions. Unless specified, decisions require a majority of votes cast. Votes requiring a 50% majority of the votes cast include, for example, decisions taken by the Executive Board pertaining to the Fund's daily function (such as approval of specific lending programs). Special majorities of 70% or 85% of total voting power (as compared to the number of votes cast) are required for decisions that fundamentally alter the IMF's operational practices. The 70% threshold applies mainly to decisions taken by the Executive Board on financial matters such as the design of IMF facilities, changes to the interest rate on IMF loans, the budget of the IMF, etc. The 85% threshold applies mainly to Board of Governor decisions on the Fund's governance structure, such as amending the IMF's Articles of Agreement and changing the number of Executive Directors. Because the U.S. vote exceeds 15% of the total voting share, no major actions can go into effect without U.S. consent. The same can be said for other major blocks of IMF member countries, principally European countries.[3]

PROPOSED REFORMS

Motivation for Reform

IMF member countries and staff have pursued reforms to address two problems facing the IMF: (1) core IMF resources have substantially declined as a share of the global economy, while anticipated needs have increased; and (2) the voice and vote of many emerging and developing countries at the IMF increasingly under-represents their current contribution to the global economy, a development which some analysts believe harms support and buy-in for IMF policies and initiatives among critical constituencies.

Adequacy of IMF Resources

Focus on the adequacy of IMF resources has been on the IMF quota, the financial commitment that countries make when they join the Fund. It has traditionally been the main source of funding that the IMF uses for financial assistance packages. It also determines a member countries' voting power at the IMF.[4] *Figure 1* shows how IMF quota resources have changed over time relative to different measures of international economic activity since 1975. In general, IMF quota resources have fallen relative to global GDP, net capital inflows, trade, and reserves in recent decades. Some analysts view this as evidence that IMF quota resources have not kept pace with increased economic integration and that the IMF needs more financial resources in order to remain effective in responding to economic crises, one of its three major functions.

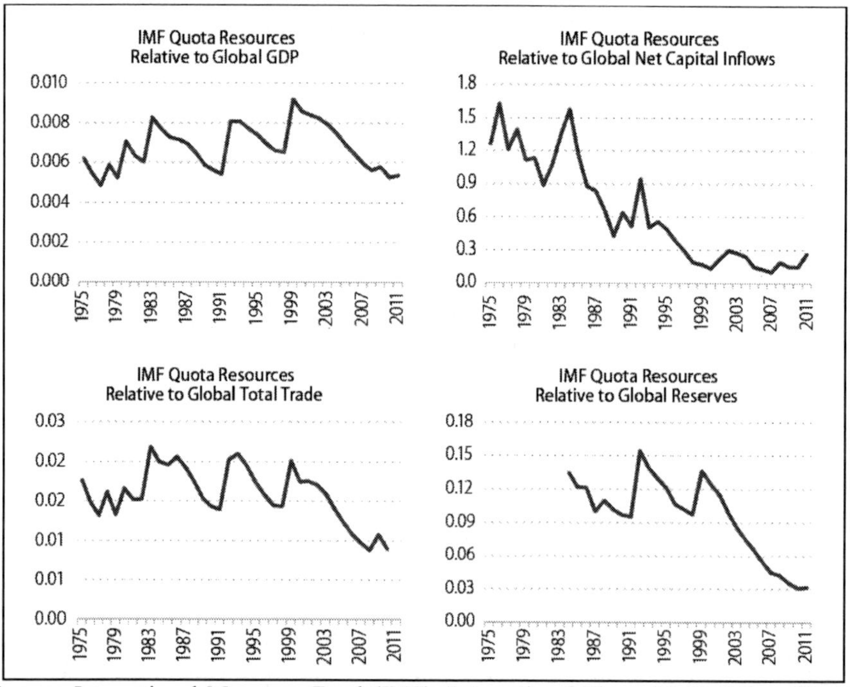

Source: International Monetary Fund (IMF), International Financial Statistics; World Bank, World Development Indicators.

Notes: Net capital inflows include portfolio investment and foreign direct investment (FDI). Reserves include holdings of gold.

Figure 1. IMF Quota Relative to International Economic Activity.

In recent years, the IMF has found ways to supplement its quota resources, which currently total about $367 billion.[5] In the wake of the global financial crisis of 2008-2009, the IMF greatly expanded a supplemental fund of resources at the IMF called the "New Arrangements to Borrow" (the NAB).[6]

Thirty-eight countries, including the United States, have committed about $570 billion to the NAB.[7] In addition, during the ongoing Eurozone crisis, 37 countries have pledged a total of $456 billion of bilateral loans to the IMF. The United States has not participated in these new bilateral pledges.[8]

Some commentators argue that having the large supplemental fund (the NAB) and large bilateral pledges are inadequate substitutes for increasing quota resources. They argue that such large supplemental funds and bilateral borrowings undermine the legitimacy of the IMF as a quota-based institution, where many crucial aspects of the organization, including access to finances and voting power, are influenced by quota. Additionally, they argue that because NAB resources are more difficult to use than quota resources, the IMF's ability to move quickly during crises is weakened.[9] Bilateral commitments may also be temporary, and may not be a reliable source of funds in the future.

Representation of Emerging and Developing Countries

In addition to concerns about the adequacy of IMF resources, some IMF members worry that the voice and vote of emerging and developing countries are "under-represented" at the IMF. This under-representation, critics argue, puts into question the evenhanded provision of IMF resources among crisis-afflicted member countries. The ability of emerging economies to influence IMF strategic policies may also be lower, potentially undermining the legitimacy of the IMF in the views of some members.

Similar concerns prompted reforms at the IMF in 2006 and 2008; however these reforms were largely seen as incremental and inadequate steps towards a meaningful solution.[10] Successive U.S. administrations have generally been supportive of increasing representation of emerging markets at the IMF. A former U.S. Alternate Executive Director to the IMF argues that on governance issues, the United States' aim was to "gain political good will for taking the lead in addressing an unfair structure that undermined the credibility and legitimacy of the IMF—an institution that the United States rightly saw as a positive benefit to itself and the world."[11]

In theory, IMF voting shares are supposed to reflect a country's relative weight in the global economy, but voting shares have proved slow to change and do not fully reflect major changes in recent decades. The increasing economic influence of Brazil, India, Russia, and China (the BRICs), for example, illustrate the changing distribution of global growth and the diffusion of economic power among a much wider group of countries than when the IMF was founded in 1944. *Figure 2* compares the share of GDP and share of

IMF quota (which affects IMF voting shares) for the BRICs and a group of advanced European economies. The share of global GDP produced by the BRICs started to increase in the mid-2000s, while the share of global GDP produced by the group of advanced European economies has fallen in recent decades. However, IMF quota share, and hence voting power, for both sets of countries has remained relatively flat.

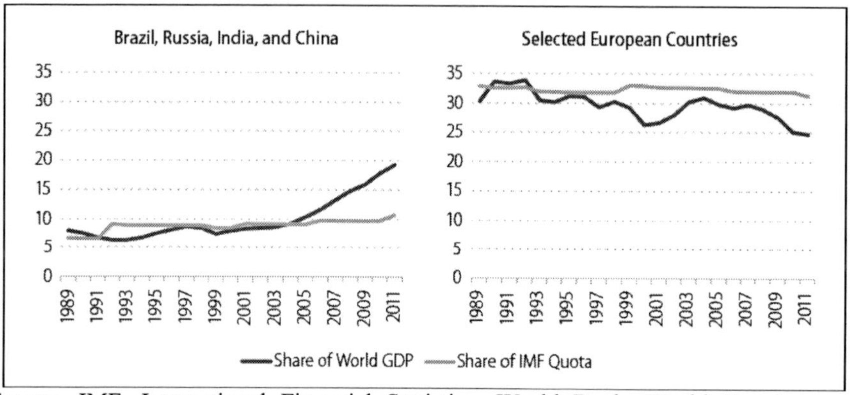

Source: IMF, International Financial Statistics; World Bank, World Development Indicators.

Notes: Countries selected for illustrative purposes only; other countries or groupings may be considered under- or over-represented at the IMF. Selected European countries include Austria, Belgium, Denmark, Finland, France, Germany, Greece, Ireland, Italy, Luxembourg, the Netherlands, Norway, Portugal, Spain, Sweden, Switzerland, and the United Kingdom.

Figure 2. IMF Quota and Share of GDP: Selected Emerging Markets and European Countries Since 1989.

Concerns about dominance of European views and interests on the IMF Executive Board have also been expressed.[12] The IMF Executive Board, which meets several times a week, has 24 members (Executive Directors), and is normally chaired by the IMF Managing Director (currently Christine Lagarde of France). *Table 1* shows the nationality of Executive Directors of the Executive Board in September 2012.[13] Eight of the 24 Executive Directors were from advanced European economies, and an additional two Executive Directors represented groups of countries that included at least one advanced European economy.

An overabundance of European Executive Directors, critics argue, limits the ability of non-European Executive Directors to represent adequately their constituencies' interests and for IMF members to hold their Executive Director accountable.

They have suggested that European voices on the Board should be consolidated, allowing for more seats on the Board to be controlled by emerging and developing countries. Several of the Executive Directors represent large constituencies of African and South American countries, many of which are among the IMF's poorest members who depend on the IMF for lending.

Table 1. Nationality of IMF Executive Directors September 2012

Executive Directors from Advanced EuropeanEconomies	Executive Directors Representing Advanced European Economies	Other Executive Directors
ermany*	anada (constituency ıdes Ireland)[1]	hited States*
ance*	exico (constituency ıdes Spain)[1]	pan*
K*		ngapore[1]
elgium[1]		hina
etherlands[1]		ıstralia[1]
ıly[1]		esotho[1]
enmark[1]		gypt[1]
vitzerland[1]		dia[1]
		azil[1]
		audi Arabia
		Russia
		ran[1]
		Argentina[1]
		Togo[1]

Source: IMF, "IMF Executive Directors and Voting Powers," Accessed September 2012, http://www.imf.org/external/np/sec/memdir/eds.aspx.

Notes: *Appointed Executive Directors; all other Executive Directors are elected.

[1] Executive Directors representing groups of countries (constituencies). Executive Directors do not have equal voting shares. A new Executive Board was formed in November 2012, with major changes. See the discussion below in "Status of Reform" for more details.

The 2010 Reform Package

In December 2010, the IMF's Board of Governors approved a package of reforms to address these concerns.[14] Key components of the reform package include:[15]

- *Doubling IMF quota and rollback of the NAB*: The reform package calls for a doubling of IMF quota, and a corresponding rollback of the NAB. Although IMF quota has been periodically increased before, if adopted, this would be the largest proportional quota increase in the history of the IMF.[16]
- *Shifting IMF quota to emerging economies:* The reform package also calls for a 6% shift in quota share to emerging markets, which would increase their voting power at the IMF, as well as their relative financial commitments to the institution. If implemented, the negotiated changes in quota shares would result in China becoming the third-largest shareholder at the IMF, and India and Brazil would also join China and Russia among the 10 largest shareholders.[17] The United States quota share would fall slightly, but the U.S. quota would still be sufficient to ensure it had more than the 15% of the total voting power needed to veto major IMF policy decisions. See *Table A-1* for more details about how IMF quota shares would change for major economies.
- *Creating an all-elected IMF Executive Board:* Rather than continuing the practice of having the five largest shareholders at the IMF appoint Executive Directors to the Board, the proposed reform would make all Executive Directors on the Executive Board elected.[18] This reform could pave the way for future consolidation of European representation on the Executive Board.[19]
- *Reducing representation of advanced European economies on the Executive Board:* Ten seats on the Executive Board represent advanced European economies. The reform proposal reflects a commitment by the membership to reduce the number of Executive Directors representing advanced European economies by two, so emerging and developing countries have more representation on the Board.

Potential Impact on the United States

If implemented, the quota reform would result in a shift in the composition of U.S. financial commitments to the IMF as the NAB is reduced and the quota is increased, but would not increase total U.S. commitments to the IMF.[20]

This shift would likely require appropriations for the entire amount of the increase but the net effect on the budget would depend on how much of the funds need to be shifted and whether there are any changes to the budgetary treatment of U.S. IMF contributions (see discussion in the "The Role of Congress" below).

Because the United States arguably has more control over when NAB funds are used compared to quota resources, the shift could entail some loss of U.S. control over the resources.[21] However, quota commitments are still generally considered very safe, and the United States has never lost money on its quota commitments (and it earns a small amount of interest on these commitments).

With the realignment of IMF quota shares towards emerging markets, the U.S. voting share would fall from 17.69% to 17.40%.[22] This change does not have a meaningful impact and would maintain the United States' unique veto power over major policy decisions at the IMF, while freeing up quota share to be shifted to emerging-market countries. The United States is actually under-represented at the IMF, with a quota share (17.69%) smaller than its share of global GDP (about 21.6% in 2011).

The United States has allowed its quota share to fall over the years, partly to facilitate realignment of IMF quota shares to reflect the increasing weight of dynamic emerging market economies in the global economy, while maintaining enough voting power to be able to veto major policy decisions at the IMF that require an 85% majority.

Since the IMF was founded, the United States has appointed its own representative to the Executive Board. Under the reform, large shareholders like the United States could still represent a constituency of one country (themselves), but other countries could in theory elect to join a large member's constituency, subject to the rules of the Fund, which aim to maintain constituencies balanced in terms of voting power.

Reducing the number of seats on the Executive Board representing advanced European economies will not impact U.S. representation on the Board.

Arguments against Reforms

Opponents of the reform argue that the IMF has sufficient resources to address financial crises, through the expansion of the NAB and through the IMF's ability to coordinate bilateral contributions during periods of intense market pressure. They also argue that the stricter process for accessing NAB funds, relative to IMF quota, is appropriate for protecting taxpayer commitments to the IMF. Moreover, some analysts reject the notion that the IMF needs more funds to combat the Eurozone crisis, because Europe has the financial resources it needs to respond to the crisis. They argue that if the IMF has any role to play in the Eurozone crisis, it should be through non-financing functions, such as through technical assistance and surveillance of economic policies and conditions.

Others are skeptical that emerging economies support the existing norms and values of international financial institutions, and question whether they would be "responsible stakeholders." Emerging countries may also have significantly different views on economic policies, such as on free markets and state-led development. There may be concerns among critics of the reform package that increasing the voice and participation of emerging markets at the IMF could result in the support of economic policies that are less aligned with the preferred policies of advanced economies.

Status of Reform

Although the IMF Board of Governors approved the reform package in 2010, some of the key parts of the package require additional action to take effect. To move to an all-elected Executive Board, three-fifths of IMF member countries representing 85% of the voting share need to formally approve an amendment to the IMF's Articles of Agreement. For the quota reform (doubling quota and shifting of quota to emerging markets) to take effect, the amendment to the Articles providing for an all-elected Executive Board must be approved, and IMF members representing at least 70% of total quotas consent to the quota changes.

With the largest voting power at the IMF (16.75%), the reforms cannot go through without U.S. support, even though a majority of IMF member countries have approved them. *Table 2* summarizes the approval process for the Board amendment and the quota reform, and the number of formal approvals received to date by the IMF.

Table 2. IMF Quota and Board Reforms: Progress to Date

Reform	Threshold of Approvals/Consents Needed	Approvals as of January 15, 2013	United States submitted formal approval to IMF?
Board Reform: Amend the IMF Articles of Agreement to create an allelected Executive Board	Three-fifths of IMF members (113 countries out of the total 188 country membership) representing 85% of the total voting power must approve amendment	130 members representing 70.24% of the total voting power	No
Quota: Double IMF quota, and shift voting power to emerging economies	Members representing 70% of total quotas must consent to quota increase, and the above proposed board reform amendment m st have entered into force	145 members representing 77.07% of the quota share Board Reform Amendment has not yet entered into force	No

Source: IMF, "Proposed Amendment on the Reform of the IMF Executive Board and Fourteenth General Review of Quotas – Status of Acceptances and Consents," January 15, 2013,http://www.imf.org/external/np/pp/eng/2013/011513.pdf.

By contrast, reducing the seats held by advanced European economies on the IMF Executive Board is a more informal process. Countries voluntarily decide how to group themselves on the Executive Board, and the consolidation will require coordination and proactive action among IMF members. The initial reform package included the pledge to reduce the representation of advanced European economies on the Executive Board by two seats following the implementation of the other reforms.[23] However, the process for obtaining the required acceptances for the Board amendment and consents to the quota reform has taken longer than expected, and steps towards Board realignment were taken in November 2012. In particular, the Belgium and Netherlands seats merged.[24]

Austria is currently serving as an Executive Director for the seat vacated by Belgium, but reportedly will rotate its chair with Turkey, the Czech Republic, and Hungary.[25]

It has also been reported that the grouping of Nordic countries will permit all the Baltic members of the group to rotate serving as the Executive Director, and that the Switzerland Executive Director will rotate with Poland in a few years.[26]

The Role of Congress

Congressional support is necessary for the United States to consent to the quota reform and accept the amendment to create an all-elected Executive Board. The Bretton Woods Act, which authorizes U.S. participation in the IMF, states that, among other things, the Administration cannot consent to a change in U.S. quota at the IMF or accept an amendment to the IMF Articles of Agreement, unless Congress authorizes such action by law.[27] Therefore, congressional action will determine the outcome of the U.S. position and, by extension, the success of the reform effort.

In addition to the congressional role in authorizing the reforms, appropriations will be necessary for the quota reform. For the United States, the reform with entail a nearly doubling of the U.S. quota at the IMF and a corresponding rollback of U.S. financial participation in the NAB. Total U.S. financial commitment to the IMF would not change. Any appropriations needed for the transfer would depend on the scoring by the Congressional Budget Office (CBO). This determination would include factors such as whether U.S. commitments to the NAB are more, less, or equally risky than U.S. commitments to quota resources.

The last time the United States increased its financial commitments to the IMF, in 2009, there was a debate over their budgetary treatment, which resulted in a change in the budgetary process that had been in place since 1980.[28] Since 1980, contributions to the IMF had been handled as an exchange of assets, which required increases in budget authority but no outlays. In 2009, it was decided that the new U.S. commitments to the IMF would be treated as lines of credit. Congress had to appropriate funds as a potential loan-loss reserve, consistent with the treatment of federal loans under the Federal Credit Reform Act (FCRA) of 1990 (P.L. 101-508), but also adjusted for market risk. The Congressional Budget Office (CBO) determined that $5 billion needed to be appropriated for the approximately $108 billion in new commitments to the IMF (P.L. 111-32).

Congressional Debate and Options for Congress

Some analysts speculated that the Administration would submit a formal request to Congress for authorizing the quota reform and amendment to the

IMF Articles to create an all-elected Executive Board in 2012, in order to help the IMF reach its goal of implementing the reforms by the October 2012 Annual Meetings. No request was made by the Administration in 2012, and no action was taken in the 112th Congress. Some speculate that the request could come in 2013 and be considered in the 113th Congress.

Some analysts are also skeptical as to the interest among Members of Congress to change the composition of U.S. commitments to the IMF. In the 112th Congress, continuing concerns about the use of IMF resources in the Eurozone debt crisis contributed to the introduction of legislation in the House and Senate (H.R. 2313, S.Amdt. 501, and S. 1276) that would rescind U.S. financial commitments to the IMF approved by Congress in 2009, primarily through to the NAB. Similar language was also included in a House draft of the FY2012 State and Foreign Operations Appropriations bill.[29]

Congress has at least four options regarding the reform package. The authorizing committees for the IMF are the Senate Committee on Foreign Relations and the House Committee on Financial Services.

Option 1: Do not Authorize U.S. Participation in the Reforms

Congress could choose not to authorize U.S. support for the reform package. Without U.S. approval, the reforms could not take effect and the current IMF funding and governance structures would not change. U.S. financial commitments at the NAB would not be transferred to IMF quota, emerging markets would not gain a greater voice at the IMF, and the United States would continue to appoint its own Executive Director. The United States would, however, face strong backlash from other IMF members for "blocking" reforms that have been approved by a majority of IMF member countries. Congress could urge the Administration to use its "voice and vote" at the IMF to pursue and negotiate a different set of reforms.

Option 2: Authorize the Administration to Accept Both Reforms

Congress could authorize both parts of the reform package: the amendment to the Articles of Agreement providing for an all-elected Board and the quota reform, and pass whatever appropriations may be needed for the quota reform. If the United States supports the reform package, the increase in the U.S. quota would be counterbalanced by an equivalent reduction of U.S. participation in the NAB, and the United States would start electing its representative to the IMF, rather than appointing its representative. Emerging markets would gain greater voting power at the IMF, and increase their relative financial commitments to the IMF. The legislation could include a reporting requirement, such as having the Administration report to Congress on how increased IMF quota resources are being used, or how increased representation of emerging markets at the IMF is shaping IMF policies.

Option 3: Authorize U.S. Support for the Board Reform, but Not the Quota Reform

Congress could authorize the Administration to accept an amendment to the Articles of Agreement providing for an all-elected Board, but not authorize U.S. participation in the quota increase. If the United States supports the Board amendment, the Executive Board would become an all-elected body and the U.S. representative would be elected, not appointed. The quota reform would also take effect, even without U.S. consent. Quota subscriptions by others could then proceed, and the U.S. quota share would decline as others implement their quota increases. Given the size of the quota increase (doubling), the U.S. quota share would be expected to fall below 15%. This would mean that the U.S. financial commitments to quota would fall relative to other countries, but that the United States would also lose its veto power in supermajority decisions requiring 85% of the voting share. For this reason, it is extremely unlikely that any administration would consent to the Board reform amendment without the quota increase.

Option 4: Authorize U.S. Support for the Quota Reform, but Not the Board Reform

Congress could authorize U.S. participation in the quota increase but not amend the Articles of Agreement to create an all-elected Board. Because quota reform is conditional on the completion of the Board reform, neither of the reforms would take effect.

CONCLUDING REMARKS

In response to concerns among IMF member nations that the institution was underfunded given the potential global needs for crisis funding and that the developing and emerging economies were underrepresented, member nations agreed in December 2010 an ambitious package of reforms. If completed, these reforms would double the IMF's quota resources and allow emerging and developing countries to own a larger share of the institution and take on more responsibility for the Fund's governance.

In order for key parts of the reform package to take effect, IMF rules dictate that the reforms must be formally accepted by three-fifths of IMF members (113 members out of 188 members) representing 85% of the total voting power. Under this formula, although unanimous support is not required, approval by the United States, the IMF's largest stakeholder is essential. To date, no action has been taken by Congress on the necessary legislation.

APPENDIX. CURRENT AND PROPOSED IMF QUOTA SHARES: TOP SHAREHOLDERS

Table A-1. Top IMF Shareholders: Current and Proposed

	Current Largest IMF Quota Shareholders		*Proposed Largest IMF Quota Shareholders*		*Largest Economies*	
	Country	IMF Quota Share	Country	IMF Quota Share	Country	% of 2011 Global GDP
1	United States	17.69%	United States	17.40%	United States	21.57%
2	Japan	6.56	Japan	6.46	China	10.44
3	Germany	6.12	China	6.39	Japan	8.39
4	France	4.51	Germany	5.58	Germany	5.16
5	UK	4.51	France	4.23	France	3.97
6	China	4.00	UK	4.23	Brazil	3.57
7	Italy	3.31	Italy	3.16	UK	3.48
8	Saudi Arabia	2.93	India	2.75	Italy	3.15
9	Canada	2.67	Russia	2.71	Russia	2.65
10	Russia	2.50	Brazil	2.32	India	2.61
11	India	2.44	Canada	2.31	Canada	2.49
12	Netherlands	2.17	Saudi Arabia	2.10	Australia	2.13
13	Belgium	1.93	Spain	2.00	Spain	2.12
14	Brazil	1.79	Mexico	1.87	Mexico	1.65
15	Spain	1.69	Netherlands	1.83	South Korea	1.60
16	Mexico	1.52	Korea	1.80	Indonesia	1.21
17	Switzerland	1.45	Australia	1.38	Netherlands	1.20
18	South Korea	1.41	Belgium	1.34	Turkey	1.11
19	Australia	1.36	Switzerland	1.21	Switzerland	0.95
20	Venezuela	1.12	Turkey	0.98	Saudi Arabia	0.85

Source: Current IMF quota shares from IMF, "IMF Members' Quota and Voting Power, and IMF Board of Governors," http://www.imf.org/external/np/sec/memdir/members.aspx; IMF quota share if reforms are implemented from IMF,

"Updated IMF Quota Data—August 2012," August 8, 2012, Table A4: Distribution of Quotas and Calculated Quotas—By Member, http://www.imf.org/external/np/fin/quotas/2012/0812.htm; Ranking by GDP from IMF, World Economic Outlook, October 2012.

Notes: GDP does not adjust for differences in price levels across countries (purchasing power parity, PPP). Using GDP adjusted for PPP would produce a different ranking, and countries disagree about which measure is more appropriate. This list is for illustrative purposes only.

End Notes

[1] For example, see Lesley Wroughton, "IMF Vote Reform Bogged Down by Delays, Deadlock," Reuters, October 8, 2012, http://www.reuters.com/article/2012/10/08/us-imf-governance-idUSBRE8970B120121008.

[2] See CRS Report RL33626, International Monetary Fund: Reforming Country Representation, by Martin A. Weiss.

[3] For example, with a combined vote greater than 15%, Germany, France, and the UK could also block a vote requiring 85% of the voting power, if the countries voted together.

[4] An IMF member's quota share and voting power are not equal since the number of a member's votes includes a set number of so-called "basic votes" provided to all members in addition to one vote for each 100,000 Special Drawing Right of IMF quota.

[5] IMF, "IMF Members' Quotas and Voting Power, and IMF Board of Governors," http://www.imf.org/external/np/sec/ memdir/members.aspx. The IMF denominates values in special drawing rights (SDRs), a basket of international currencies. In this report, values denominated in SDRs are converted to U.S. dollars using the exchange rate on October 15, 2012: 1 SDR = $1.54 (Source: IMF). However, dollar amounts should be viewed as approximations, as fluctuations in the exchange rate change the precise value in dollars.

[6] For details about U.S. legislation that increased the U.S. financial commitment to the NAB, see CRS Report R40578, The Global Financial Crisis: Increasing IMF Resources and the Role of Congress, by Jonathan E. Sanford and Martin A. Weiss.

[7] IMF, "IMF Standing Borrowing Arrangements," http://www.imf.org/external/np/exr/facts/gabnab.htm.

[8] IMF, "IMF Managing Director Christine Lagarde Welcomes Additional Pledges to Increase IMF Resources, Bringing Total Commitments to US$456 Billion," June 19, 2012, http://www.imf.org/external/np/sec/pr/2012/pr12231.htm.

[9] Quota resources can be used to fund a new program with a simple majority vote on the Executive Board. In contrast, NAB resources can only be used to fund programs when the NAB has been "activated," for a period of up to 6 months. The NAB can only be activated if a proposal by the IMF Managing Director to activate the NAB is accepted by participants representing 85% of total NAB commitments and is then approved by a simple majority of the Executive Board. Once the NAB has been "activated," NAB resources are combined with quota resources, and use of the resources to fund a new program requires a simple majority vote of the Executive Board.

[10] For more on previous efforts to increase the vote and participation of emerging and developing countries, see CRS Report RL33626, International Monetary Fund: Reforming Country Representation, by Martin A. Weiss.

[11] Douglas Rediker, "Losing at the IMF," Foreign Policy, October 10, 2012, http://www.foreignpolicy.com/articles/ 2012/10/10/losing_at_the_imf.

[12] "The Case for IMF Quota Reform," Council on Foreign Relations Expert Roundup, October 11, 2012, http://www.cfr.org/imf/case-imf-quota-reform/p29248.

[13] A new Executive Board formed in November 2012, which is discussed in greater detail later in the report (see "Status of Reform").

[14] IMF, "IMF Board of Governors Approves Major Quota and Governance Reforms," December 16, 2010, http://www.imf.org/external/np/sec/pr/2010/pr10477.htm; and IMF, "Selected Decisions and Selected Documents of the IMF, Thirty-Fifth Issue – Fourteenth General Review of Quotas and Reform of the Executive Board," http://www.imf.org/external/pubs/ ft/sd/index.asp?decision=66-2.

[15] This report focuses on components of the reform package that require specific congressional action to implement, are the most proximate, and/or have been the most controversial. Other components of the reform package relating to quotas include a comprehensive review of the quota formula by January 2013 and another general review of quotas by January 2014, which would further enhance the voice of emerging markets at the IMF. Other components of the reform package relating to the Executive Board include allowing more Executive Directors to appoint a second alternate Executive Director; maintaining the current 24 seats on the Executive Board (instead of the 20-seat Board originally outlined in the IMF Articles, subject to increase or decrease by the Board of Governors); and reviewing the composition of the Executive Board every eight years.

[16] The second-largest proportional increase in IMF quota was by 60.7% in 1958-1959. For all IMF quota increases, see "General Quota Reviews" at IMF, "IMF Quotas," http://www.imf.org/external/np/exr/facts/quotas.htm.

[17] IMF, "IMF Quotas," http://www.imf.org/external/np/exr/facts/quotas.htm.

[18] The United States would still retain its single seat on the Executive Board.

[19] Countries currently form groups voluntarily, typically on the basis of geographical or historical affinity. A few countries—China, Russia, and Saudi Arabia—have enough votes to elect their own Executive Directors. For the composition of the current Executive Board, see http://www.imf.org/external/np/sec/memdir/eds.aspx.

[20] Currently, the United States has committed about $65 billion to IMF quota and about $106 billion to the NAB.

[21] NAB resources can only be used to fund programs when the NAB has been "activated." The United States can veto activation of the NAB. By contrast, a simple majority of the Executive Board can approve using quota resources to fund a program; the United States cannot veto use of quota resources.

[22] IMF, "Executive Board Approves Major Overhaul of Quotas and Governance," November 5, 2012, http://www.imf.org/external/np/sec/pr/2010/pr10418.htm.

[23] IMF, "Selected Decisions and Selected Documents of the IMF, Thirty-Fifth Issue – Fourteenth General Review of Quotas and Reform of the Executive Board," http://www.imf.org/external/pubs/ft/sd/index.asp?decision=66-2.

[24] For details about the Executive Board that formed on November 1, 2012, see http://www.imf.org/external/np/sec/memdir/eds.aspx.

[25] Sandrine Rastello, "IMF Board Sees Biggest Power Shift Reshuffle in Two Decades," Bloomberg, October 14, 2012, http://www.businessweek.com/news/2012-10-14/imf-board-sees-biggest-power-shift-reshuffle-in-two-decades.

[26] Ibid.

[27] 22 U.S.C. 286c.

[28] For more on the budgetary treatment of U.S. contributions to the IMF, see the Appendix in CRS Report R40578, The Global Financial Crisis: Increasing IMF Resources and the Role of Congress, by Jonathan E. Sanford and Martin A. Weiss. For more on the 2009 debate, see CBO, "Budget Implications of U.S. Contributions to the International Monetary Fund," CBO Blog post, May 19, 2009, http://www.cbo.gov/publication/24901.

[29] A copy of the draft bill is available on the House Appropriations website, http://appropriations.house.gov/ UploadedFiles/FY12-SFOPS-07-25_xml.pdf.

In: International Monetary Fund
Editor: Juan A. Dumas

ISBN: 978-1-62808-288-3

Chapter 3

EGYPT AND THE IMF: OVERVIEW AND ISSUES FOR CONGRESS*

Rebecca M. Nelson and Jeremy M. Sharp

SUMMARY

Congress, which annually oversees and appropriates $1.55 billion in bilateral foreign aid to Egypt, is following the political and economic situation in Egypt closely. Economic conditions in Egypt have deteriorated rapidly since the 2011 "revolution." Political uncertainty abruptly reduced foreign capital flows into Egypt; growth, while still positive, has slowed substantially; the central bank is at risk of running out of foreign exchange reserves; and unemployment has increased from 9.2% before the revolution to 12.3% in 2012.

Many policymakers and analysts fear that the fragile economic conditions in Egypt jeopardize the country's political transition and broader stability in the region.

Egyptian authorities and the International Monetary Fund (IMF) have been in negotiations for more than two years over an IMF loan to Egypt in exchange for policy reforms that, if successful, could stave off economic collapse and create more "inclusive" growth. The IMF reached

---

* This is an edited, reformatted and augmented version of a Congressional Research Service publication, CRS Report for Congress R43053, from www.crs.gov, prepared for Members and Committees of Congress, dated April 29, 2013.

tentative agreements with first the military-controlled Supreme Council of the Armed Forces (SCAF) in June 2011 and later with Egyptian President Mohammed Morsi in November 2012. The November 2012 program would have provided $4.8 billion in assistance, and other donors pledged about $9.7 billion in additional financing once the IMF program was in place. No agreement has been finalized or implemented to date.

Egyptian authorities have been reluctant to commit to economic reforms that may be politically unpopular and increase the country's debt. Pressure to cut fuel subsidies is a particular issue. More broadly, many Egyptians associate the IMF programs in the late 1980s and 1990s with adverse social outcomes. On its part, the IMF has resisted a program that does not have sufficient conditionality consistent with its lending policies. Continuing political concerns and uncertainty in Egypt have also contributed to the delay. In the absence of an IMF agreement, the Egyptian government has recently secured financial support from Libya and Qatar.

Issues for Congress

Some lawmakers who oppose ongoing U.S. bilateral assistance to Egypt may oppose any existing or future IMF support of Egypt, on several potential grounds. Some may be concerned that in the rush to stabilize Egypt, the Administration could be too lenient in terms of the reforms it seeks from the Egyptian government. Others may not want the Administration to overly politicize an IMF loan. They fear that the application of too much pressure on the Morsi government could make accepting a possibly unpopular IMF deal too politically controversial to pursue and that the lack of IMF involvement in Egypt could undermine U.S. interests in the region.

The United States makes the single largest financial commitment to the IMF, and, with the largest voting power at the IMF, the United States wields a high degree of influence over IMF decisions. If Congress wanted to shape U.S. policy toward Egypt at the IMF, it could pass a "legislative mandate" legislation directing the U.S. representative at the IMF to use its "voice and vote" to push for certain policies toward Egypt at the IMF.

Lawmakers may also want to use the terms of IMF conditions as "benchmarks" for the provision of existing or new bilateral economic aid to Egypt.

Congressional concerns about bilateral debt relief are, in part, related to the absence of an IMF agreement. Additionally, legislative language (S.Amdt. 44) proposed in March 2013, but not adopted, would have tied U.S. bilateral economic assistance to Egypt to, among other things, an IMF program.

INTRODUCTION

After more than two years of social unrest and economic stagnation following the 2011 popular uprising, the government of Egypt is facing serious economic pressures that, if not remedied, could lead to economic collapse and possibly new levels of violence.

The International Monetary Fund (IMF) has been in negotiation with the government of Egypt for at least $4.8 billion in loans in exchange for structural economic reforms, such as subsidy reduction. Egyptian acceptance of an IMF loan could also pave the way for billions more in financial assistance from other bilateral and multilateral donors, potentially providing Egypt with time to stabilize its political system and economy. The Obama Administration is encouraging President Mohammed Morsi to reach out to the opposition and the public in order to gain the political support to quickly reach a deal with the IMF in order to stave off further economic uncertainty. Egyptian leaders are concerned about the political ramifications of required IMF reforms, which could be politically unpopular.

Congress, which annually oversees and appropriates $1.55 billion in bilateral foreign aid to Egypt, is following the situation in Egypt closely, including the Islamist-led government's stated commitment to, among other things, pursuing democratic principles and continued peace with Israel. Some Members of Congress are also closely monitoring Egypt-IMF negotiations. U.S. funds to provide bilateral debt relief to Egypt have been tied to Egypt committing to an economic program in conjunction with the IMF. Legislative language also has been proposed that would tie U.S. bilateral economic assistance to Egypt to, among other things, an IMF program and implementation of reforms under the program. Congress could also pass legislation to shape U.S. policy toward Egypt at the IMF. More generally, in the 113th Congress, lawmakers have proposed a number of bills that would prohibit, restrict, or rescind bilateral U.S. assistance and/or arms sales to Egypt.[1]

This report provides an overview of the economic situation in post-revolution Egypt and negotiations between Egypt and the IMF. It also analyzes why an IMF program is controversial in Egypt and the relationship between an IMF program for Egypt and U.S. foreign policy goals in the region. It discusses the IMF program from a congressional perspective, including how debt relief for Egypt has been tied to an IMF program and legislation that would condition U.S. bilateral economic assistance to Egypt on an IMF program.

BACKGROUND

Deteriorating Economic Conditions in Post-Revolution Egypt

Economic conditions in Egypt have gradually deteriorated since the 2011 revolution, potentially exacerbating an already polarized Egyptian political climate. Neither military nor civilian authorities have been able to restore confidence in the economy. Continued insecurity stemming from deterioration in law and order has hampered investment. The Islamist-led government and the opposition have blamed each other for worsening economic conditions, and while Egypt has not reached a crisis "tipping point," there is some concern that economic shocks, such as a dramatic currency devaluation or sudden steep rise in the cost of living, could lead to street violence.

Before the political changes began taking shape, Egypt's economy was strong in many respects. The economy was growing at a fairly rapid pace, averaging 5% a year between 2000 and 2010.[2] Starting in 2004, the government pursued wide-ranging structural reforms, including tariff reductions, privatization of state-owned enterprises, and reductions in regulation of the private sector, among other policy measures, that aimed to improve the business environment and make Egypt's economy more competitive.[3] The 2008 World Bank *Doing Business* report ranked Egypt as the top worldwide economic reformer.[4] In general, reforms helped attract foreign capital, and foreign direct investment (FDI) in Egypt surged from 1.2% of GDP in 2000 to 9.3% of GDP in 2006. The global financial crisis of 2008-2009 had limited impact on Egypt's economy, due to low exposure to the types of structured financial products at the heart of the financial crisis and the government's accommodating fiscal and monetary policies following the onset of the crisis.

Behind strong growth and capital inflows during the 2000s, however, Egypt's economy faced a number of vulnerabilities. Average Egyptians saw little immediate benefit from the economic reforms praised by outside observers and investors. Growth had done little to lower persistently high unemployment, which averaged 9.9% during the 2000s (and was reportedly much higher among youth), or substantially reduce poverty. Fifteen percent of the population, or about one in seven Egyptians, were living on less than $2 per day in 2008. The government was also running relatively large budget deficits, averaging 8.2% of GDP between 2002 and 2010. In its 2010 annual review of Egypt's economy, the IMF cautioned about the need for fiscal consolidation and recommended a value-added tax (VAT), energy subsidy reform, and measures to contain the fiscal cost of pension and health reforms.[5] Persistent budget deficits also left public debt at 73% of GDP in 2010, above the 60% threshold that some economists believe is stable and conducive to growth. The IMF also warned about the need to continue reform "momentum" to further improve the business environment and build the private sector. Finally, inflation had steadily increased through the decade, from 2.8% in 2000 to 11.7% in 2008.[6]

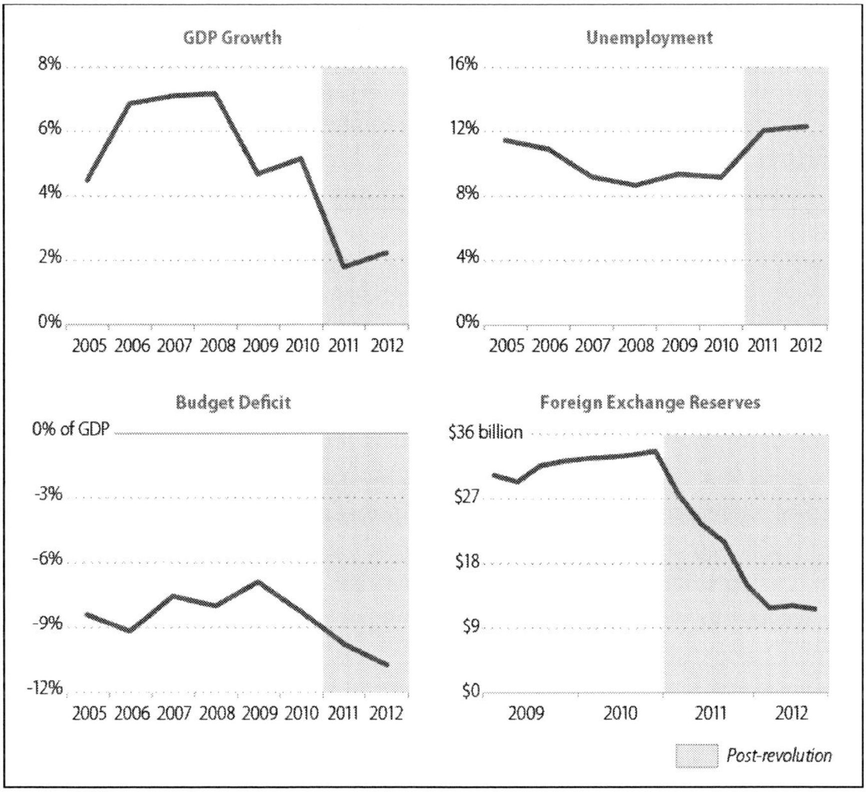

Source: IMF, World Economic Outlook, April 2013; IMF, International Financial Statistics, 2013

Figure 1. Economic Challenges in Post-Revolution Egypt.

The revolution in Egypt unraveled the conditions underpinning growth in the 2000s and brought potential vulnerabilities to the forefront. The revolution and ensuing political uncertainty eroded investor confidence, triggering a sharp reduction in capital inflows and an abrupt decline in tourism revenue, on which many jobs depend.[7] Economic growth fell to 1.8% in 2011 and 2.2% in

2012. Unemployment rose from 9.2% in 2010 to 12.3% in 2012. The new Egyptian authorities, brought to power in elections in mid-2012 as the military regime that took power in early 2011 formally stepped aside, retreated from previous pledges for fiscal consolidation, and the budget deficit widened from 7.8% of GDP in 2010 to 11.2% in 2012. General economic trends in Egypt before and after the revolution are depicted above, in *Figure 1.*

The Morsi government has been reluctant to reduce fuel subsidies, and has continued to earmark a large proportion of fiscal expenditures for social spending, seemingly as a means for securing continued political support.[8] The government has also increasingly relied on domestic markets to finance the deficit, which is more expensive than borrowing on international markets and has further strained government finances. Public debt rose from 73% of GDP in 2010 to 80% in 2012.

Political uncertainty and capital outflows have also reduced demand for Egypt's currency, the Egyptian pound, resulting in pressure on the Egyptian pound to depreciate. The Egyptian central bank generally does not allow its currency to be determined entirely by market forces (i.e., to float freely, like the U.S. dollar), and has been selling foreign exchange reserves in an attempt to manage a gradual depreciation. The central bank's holdings of foreign exchange reserves fell from $34 billion in the fourth quarter of 2010 to $12 billion in 2012, a level that many economists fear puts the central bank at risk of running out of reserves and triggering a currency crisis.[9] The central bank has also increased interest rates to stem pressure on the pound, which some economists fear undermines the government's growth objectives in the short-term. A depreciated local currency means that Egyptian households' wealth and wages are worth less in terms of purchasing power, as imported goods become more expensive.

Egypt-IMF Negotiations

With slowing growth, rising unemployment, dwindling foreign exchange reserves, and a growing budget deficit, many economists argue that Egypt faces two broad economic challenges: (1) sustaining macroeconomic stability in the short-term; and (2) implementing economic reforms in the medium-term to deliver growth to broad segments of society ("inclusive growth"), foster private sector development, and create jobs.

The IMF is in a position to help stabilize Egypt's economy and, potentially, advance reform efforts. The IMF provides loans to countries facing economic crises, and its short-term loans (typically disbursed over one- to three-years) can ensure continuous access to affordable financing, providing the government with breathing space to implement needed economic reforms. IMF loans are disbursed in phases ("tranches"), contingent upon the implementation of economic reforms, which have been negotiated between the government and the IMF at the onset of the program ("conditionality"). Targets may be revisited, however, over the course of the program in response to changing economic conditions.[10] Other Arab countries in "transition" are facing similar pressures, and the IMF has negotiated and started programs in Jordan, Morocco, Tunisia, and Yemen.

Egyptian authorities and the IMF have been in on-again, off-again negotiations essentially since political changes started taking shape in Egypt. Two tentative ("staff-level") agreements were reached, in June 2011 and November 2012, but no agreement has been finalized or implemented. Egyptian authorities have been reluctant to commit to economic reforms that may be politically unpopular and ultimately saddle the economy with more debt. A particular source of concern are fuel subsidies, which many economists view as inefficient and regressive but constitute a financial safety net for many Egyptian households. In turn, the IMF's lending policies prevent it from pursuing a program that does not have adequate conditionality commitments in place.

Continuing political concerns and uncertainty in Egypt have also contributed to the delay. In the absence of an IMF deal, Egyptian authorities are increasingly turning to other countries in the region for financial assistance, such as Libya and Qatar (described in greater detail below). However, funds from other governments may only provide a bridging mechanism and could fail to ensure that Egyptian authorities address underlying structural challenges.

Tentative Deal #1: June 2011

At the time of the first staff-level agreement, in June 2011,[11] the military-controlled Supreme Council of the Armed Forces (SCAF), led by Field Marshal Mohamed Hussein Tantawi, was exercising executive authority in Egypt and therefore negotiating with the IMF. Tantawi rejected the proposed $3.2 billion IMF loan, reportedly because he was hesitant to burden Egypt with what he considered was too much foreign debt and perhaps believing that Egypt could receive short-term loans or grants from Gulf Arab countries instead.[12] Many economists have since suggested that the terms of the June 2011 staff-level agreement would have been far less onerous in terms of conditionality than subsequent proposals; as economic conditions in Egypt continued to deteriorate in coming months, the size of the IMF program for Egypt, and the reforms attached to it, have become more ambitious.[13]

The June 2011 staff-level deal was reached before the Muslim Brotherhood began to wield real political power in post-Mubarak Egypt, but the party generally applauded the SCAF's rejection of IMF assistance as an assertion of Egyptian sovereignty, while being careful not to rule out any future multilateral lending. According to one Muslim Brotherhood communiqué published after the SCAF's rejection of the $3.2 billion IMF loan:

> The Egyptian government has adopted a new policy to strike a balance when dealing with international financing institutions. It has recently refused to finance the deficit through loans loaded with political and economic conditions. The importance of this policy is that it signals that the authorities are reconsidering ensuring the independence of the state, which is consistent with the aspirations of the revolution, to get rid of the inherited dependency of the old regime. Regardless of the methods of handling the issue and covering the budget deficit, this step would recast the Egyptian relationship with the IMF and the World Bank, which would require a great deal of effort directed at achieving stability, development, production, self-reliance and the development of our local resources. This approach also delivers a clear message to international financial institutions regarding the need to move from an era of political loans that have supported many authoritarian governments, and shifting towards taking into account more balanced relations in the new era, which would be based on the interests of the states and safeguarding their economic development.[14]

Tentative Deal #2: November 2012

Following the 2011-2012 parliamentary elections that enabled the Muslim Brotherhood's Freedom and Justice Party to form a majority coalition, Islamists assumed partial control over governance amidst a worsening economic crisis. Though the SCAF still maintained executive authority in the first half of 2012, the Brotherhood insisted that it would not support any new IMF deal unless a new, more broadly-based government was formed of which it would presumably be a part. In March 2012, Saudi Arabia reportedly deposited $1 billion in Egypt's central bank, which eased some of the immediate pressure on the Egyptian government to secure financing from the IMF quickly.[15] Egypt also reportedly received financial assistance from Qatar.

Months later, former Brotherhood leader Mohammed Morsi became president and wrested most day-to-day executive authority from the SCAF. Islamists also controlled the upper house of parliament (the lower house having been dissolved by the courts pending new elections). A second staff-level agreement was reached between Egypt and the IMF in November 2012, to provide a 22-month, $4.8 billion loan program.[16] Reaching an agreement with the IMF was also expected to unlock funds from other bilateral and multilateral donors. It is not uncommon for other donors to wait until an IMF program is in place, which can serve as a seal of approval for the government's economic policies and provide greater assurance that assistance would be used by the government wisely. The total financing package, including funds from the IMF, was reportedly $14.5 billion in loans and deposits on relatively favorable terms (compared to borrowing on the private debt market).

At the time, the government was planning on reducing spending, primarily by cutting energy subsidies, and boosting revenue, including through reforms to move from a general sales tax to a value-added tax. Possibly to demonstrate good will, the government lifted subsidies on 95-octane petrol in line with the plan in November 2012.[17] The program likely included other policy measures as well; specifics would have been released publicly when the program was finalized. One analyst expected the IMF "to ask Egypt to do all the things that the IMF always asks a country to do, which is to get its fiscal house in order; increase taxes, reduce the budget deficit, get rid of subsidies so that it can bring down inflation, do other things that will boost growth, and then get Egypt back on some kind of path toward recovery."[18]

In December 2012, public outcry erupted over the proposed tax increases, causing the government to reverse course. The Egyptian finance minister requested a delay in the program, and, eventually the government postponed the program until after the parliamentary elections, which were to end in June 2013.

Current Status

By the spring of 2013, with the economic situation still unstable, it appeared that the government would not be able to wait on IMF assistance until parliamentary elections were completed. The elections have been put on hold, possibly until the fall of 2013, due to judicial review of the electoral law. In the meantime, President Morsi has attempted to replace hundreds of judges who he believes are obstructing his agenda. Moreover, ensuring broad Egyptian public support for an IMF loan, a goal sought by many IMF members, seemed distant at best, as trust between President Morsi and his opponents had deteriorated significantly in prior months.

In March 2013, the IMF suggested that Egypt could qualify for emergency short-term financing from the IMF to stave off imminent economic collapse. Assistance would have taken the form of a bridge loan, smaller and shorter-term than the programs previously negotiated between the IMF and Egypt. It would have provided about $700 million, substantially smaller than the $4.8 billion previously on the table, but would have not come with the same conditions attached to more standard (non-emergency) loan facilities. This support could have provided Egypt with much-needed short-term cash to get through the elections, while providing the government with time to negotiate a more traditional, longer-term IMF program. However, the Morsi government eventually ruled out such emergency assistance. One Western diplomat reportedly said that the rejection of emergency financing by the government was an attempt to "bully the Fund to giving Egypt the loan."[19] Likewise, Steven Cook of the Council on Foreign Relations has cautioned that "Egypt will likely get the aid it needs to keep the country afloat, but the way they have gone about securing this assistance suggests a misplaced arrogance.... the Egyptians should dispense with their implicit 'give it to us or else' approach. Whether they like it or not, donors are not going to hand over cash without any terms."[20]

In contrast, President Morsi reportedly argued that it had "done what was required" for a longer-term IMF program and had prepared a program of reforms.[21] Reforms announced in early 2013 include, for example, elimination of energy subsidies for industrial firms over a three-year period, increases in the price of wheat, and implementation of a progressive property tax on large properties.[22] Reforms were also announced to protect the most vulnerable segments of society, including plans to implement universal health care and, for low-income families, raising the minimum tax exemption and increase social security pensions).[23] The reforms have not been without political costs. For example, the government's plans for bread subsidy reforms resulted in bakeries across Egypt threatening to shut down.[24]

Meanwhile, the Obama Administration has stressed the urgency facing Egypt with regard to an IMF program, and regarding economic and political conditions more broadly. On April 2, 2013, Secretary of State John Kerry remarked, "We share a very real concern in the Obama Administration about the direction that Egypt is apparently moving in.... We have been working very, very hard in the last weeks to try to get the government of Egypt to reach out to the opposition, to deal with the IMF, to come to an agreement which will allow Egypt to begin to transform its economy and improve the lives of its citizens."[25]

While negotiations with the IMF continued, the Egyptian government reportedly received pledges for financial support in April 2013 from Libya ($2 billion deposit to the central bank) and Qatar ($3 billion purchase of government bonds).[26] A list of selected bilateral financial assistance to Egypt is provided in *Table 1*. Some analysts believe that financial support from neighboring countries could again delay an IMF program, while others argue that this assistance could be the start of a broader financial assistance program, which includes IMF funding.[27]

Table 1. Select Budget and Central Bank Support to Egypt

Country	Date	Type and Amount of Aid
Qatar	April 2013	$3 billion loan
Libya	April 2013	$2 billion in central bank deposits
United States	March 2013	$190 million cash transfer (for debt relief)
Qatar	January 2013	$2.5 billion total (of which $2 billion loan, $500 million grant)
Turkey	September 2012	$2 billion loan
Qatar	July 2012	$2 billion in central bank deposits
Saudi Arabia	May 2012	$1 billion in central bank deposits, $750 million credit line for oil imports
Saudi Arabia	November 2011	$500 million grant
Qatar	October 2011	$500 million grant

Sources: Analysis of new reports announcing financial support to Egypt.

Notes: List may not be exhaustive, and it is not always clear to what extent announcements of financial support were fully met or re-pledged at later dates. In addition, various media sources report that the Egyptian government is seeking, or has sought, aid from other countries such as Iraq ($4 billion requested), Algeria ($2 billion), Russia, and the Arab Monetary Fund. In 2011, the UAE pledged $3 billion in various aid to Egypt, but the funds were not transferred. In April 2013, Iran offered to loan Egypt $1 billion.

By mid-April, Egypt's latest round of talks with the IMF ended without an agreement. Reportedly, the IMF stated that Egypt has taken "valuable first steps" to address energy subsidies, and that the Egyptian authorities "intend to build on these steps with further actions to address, in a socially-balanced way, the country's fiscal and balance of payments deficits, and create conditions for sustained recovery of the economy." It is not clear when talks will resume.[28]

Meanwhile, spending on fuel subsidies has increased by 40% from the previous fiscal year, largely due to a steady decline in the Egyptian pound.[29]

Stopgap funding from Qatar and Libya may allow Egypt to "muddle through" until later in the year, perhaps after parliamentary elections. By late April 2013, some economists began predicting that Egypt could avoid a fiscal crisis until late 2013. According to former finance minister Samir Radwan, "They [the Morsi government] go through the motions of pretending they are serious about an IMF deal, but actually they are not."[30] U.S. officials continue to emphasize the importance of an IMF deal, but may be frustrated by Egypt's inability to reach a deal. In recent testimony before the Senate Appropriations Subcommittee on State, Foreign Operations and Related Programs, Secretary Kerry remarked that:

> Egypt is more of a question mark right now. I mean, I'll just tell you, there are a lot of ifs about Egypt at this moment. And we've been working very, very hard with the Egyptian government to try to bring them to a point where they're prepared to embrace important reforms that are key to the IMF money, to be more inclusive with the opposition, to build out civil society, to live up to their promises regarding democracy, and it's a question mark whether they're going to make the right choices. And I can't frame it any other way for you now.[31]

Egyptian Politics and IMF Assistance

Many Egyptians view the history of modern Egypt as characterized by a long and painful legacy of the state being beholden to foreign powers, including the Ottoman Empire, European colonizers, and the United States. The narrative of colonialism and anti-imperialism permeates Egyptian political discourse and is particularly potent on issues of foreign lending and assistance. The IMF in particular is a controversial institution in Egypt, largely due to the popular association of IMF programs with autocratic rule under the Mubarak regime, and a common belief that IMF programs directly led to the rise of unemployment, poverty, inequality, and corruption (see *text box*).

Egypt and the IMF: Experience in the 1980s and 1990s

Egypt had four lending programs with the IMF in the late 1980s and 1990s, with commitments totaling about $1.7 billion. The programs focused on macroeconomic stability, including a large fiscal adjustment, an exchange rate anchor, conservative monetary policies, and moves toward liberalizing interest and exchange rate markets. The programs, particularly in the1990s, also included structural adjustment measures, such as privatization, trade liberalization, and deregulation, among other measures. From the IMF's perspective, policies aimed at macroeconomic stabilization were successful, producing "a remarkable turnaround in Egypt's macroeconomic fortunes in terms of reducing inflation, restoring confidence, and engendering external viability."[32] Egypt's efforts at structural adjustment are viewed more widely as less successful, although there is disagreement on why they failed to achieve the intended goals. Some analysts argue that the Mubarak regime did not commit strongly enough to the policy reforms, for example, by eventually largely abandoning privatization efforts due to fears of rising unemployment.[33] Other analysts argue that the government did implement reform efforts, but they came with high social costs, leading to mass layoffs of public workers, a more limited role for unions, and growing inequality.[34]

Older Egyptians from the middle and lower classes may have particularly high disregard for the IMF, as many associate reductions in their standard of living and political freedoms with IMF-mandated reductions in government spending and privatization. The IMF's lack of credibility with large segments of Egyptians has contributed to the reluctance of new leaders in Egypt to pursue a program.[35] One historian notes how former President Mubarak's government was acutely aware of the popular opposition to Egyptian acceptance of IMF reforms in the early 1990s:

> In the eyes of the regime, the economic reforms were a potential source of trouble not only because they led, or could lead, to material losses for a large part of the population; they were also potentially dangerous in that a considerable part of 'public opinion,' influenced by the dominant discourse of the past, considered them irreconcilable with the social and political achievements of the [1952] revolution and with their own interests.[36]

At present, it is difficult to gauge the extent of anti-IMF sentiment in Egypt. Although opposition to any Egyptian dealings with the IMF exists, most Egyptians are not necessarily blaming foreign lenders for their poor economy—yet. To date, small-scale protests have occurred outside the Egyptian stock exchange with protestors chanting that IMF support is akin to "economic colonialism."[37] Islamists, including hard-line Salafists, at times also have expressed reservations over accepting IMF support, arguing that Islamic law bans the payment of interest on loans. Egyptian leftists—who currently constitute the backbone of political opposition to Morsi—have been the most vocal opponents of IMF credit. They are led by third-place finisher in the 2012 presidential election, Hamdeen Sabahi, who has denounced the IMF loan on his Facebook page. Some analysts believe that there is widespread public apathy toward the IMF, with a poll conducted in August 2012 showing that only two-thirds of Egyptians were aware of the IMF loan under discussion.[38]

During an IMF delegation visit to Egypt in mid-April 2013, fund representatives held meetings with various opposition figures and political parties, including Amr Moussa, Amr Hamzawy, Mohamed ElBaradei, the Wafd party, and Hamdeen Sabahi. Reportedly, these political figures voiced various demands, including calls for greater transparency in government-IMF negotiations, and concerns, such as the burden IMF-mandated reforms would pose for the average citizen.[39]

Egypt, the IMF, and U.S. Foreign Policy Goals

The Obama Administration has supported IMF involvement in Egypt, arguing that it promotes economic reforms in Egypt and would stabilize the economy and facilitate democratic transition. The Administration has encouraged President Morsi to reach out to the opposition and the public in order to garner political support to quickly reach a deal with the IMF. In April 2013, Treasury Secretary Jacob Lew expressed support for an IMF loan to Egypt, and explicitly stated that "It would be very much in the United States' best interests for Egypt to be on a more sustainable course."[40] Likewise, in a March 2013 visit to Cairo, Secretary of State John Kerry remarked that:

> In all my meetings, I conveyed a simple but serious message: The brave Egyptians who stood vigil in Tahrir Square did not risk their lives to see that opportunity for a brighter future squandered. The Egyptian people must come together to address their economic challenge. I encouraged President Morsi to implement the homegrown reforms that will help his country secure an IMF agreement, put Egypt on the path to establishing a firm economic foundation and allow it to chart its own course. He agreed and said that he plans to move quickly to do so.... The United States can and wants to do more. Reaching an agreement with the

> IMF will require further effort on the part of the Egyptian government and broad support for reform by all Egyptians. When Egypt takes the difficult steps to strengthen its economy and build political unity and justice, we will work with our Congress at home on additional support. These steps will also unlock much-needed private-sector investment and broader financial assistance.[41]

More broadly, however, there is debate within Washington over whether an IMF deal (among other things) is an opportunity, or not, for the United States to exert influence over the Islamist-led government of Egypt to pursue policies in line with U.S. interests and values. Some argue that Egypt's need for external assistance presents the United States, which has the largest financial stake and voting power in the IMF, with an opportunity to condition U.S. support for Egypt at the IMF on the government's commitment to, among other things, pursuing democratic principles and continued peace with Israel. Some analysts are especially concerned that President Morsi, a former Muslim Brotherhood leader, appears to be consolidating power at the expense of non-Islamist political forces—behavior that they believe the Obama Administration should signal is unacceptable. These advocates suggest that U.S. support for an IMF deal amidst perceived rising Islamist autocracy would be a setback for democracy in post-Mubarak Egypt. According to Egypt experts Robert Kagan (Brookings) and Michele Dunne (Atlantic Council):

> The United States made a strategic error for years by coddling Mubarak, and his refusal to carry out reforms produced the revolution of Tahrir Square. We repeat the error by coddling Morsi at this critical moment. The United States needs to use all its options—military aid, economic aid and U.S. influence with the IMF and other international lenders—to persuade Morsi to compromise with secular politicians and civil-society leaders on political and human rights issues to rebuild security and get the economy on track.[42]

On the other hand, some observers suggest that the United States should not push Egypt too hard in its negotiations with the IMF, arguing that Egypt is "too big to fail"—from a political and an economic standpoint (Egypt has the largest population of any country in the Middle East and North Africa [about 83 million]).[43] Proponents of an IMF deal assert that if economic collapse were to occur there, the consequences for global, regional, and U.S. national security would be severe. Examples of U.S. security interests in Egypt could include access to the Suez Canal for global commerce and U.S. naval vessels;

Egypt's 35-year-old peace treaty with Israel; and U.S.- Egyptian and Egyptian-Israeli military and intelligence cooperation.

Moreover, opponents of stringent conditionality assert that any Egyptian government acceptance of IMF-mandated reforms would be politically painful enough; additional behind-the-scenes U.S. political pressure on President Morsi could unintentionally push him to seek financial aid from other, non-Western sources. Egyptian authorities have already received financial support from Saudi Arabia, Libya, and Qatar. It is unclear whether the Gulf countries support an IMF program for Egypt, and whether they are willing to commit to similar funding levels. It is also unclear what implicit or explicit political or economic conditions would be attached to financial assistance from neighboring countries in the absence of IMF involvement, and whether these conditions would be in line with U.S. interests.

ISSUES AND OPTIONS FOR CONGRESS

Considering U.S. Policy Toward Egypt at the IMF

Congress may reflect the bifurcated views identified above over the optimal U.S. policy toward Egypt at the IMF. Some lawmakers who oppose ongoing U.S. bilateral assistance to Egypt may oppose any existing or future IMF support of Egypt. For other lawmakers who may support existing aid to Egypt, the prospect of additional support to Egypt, either through the IMF, bilateral aid, or both, poses several potential concerns. First, some may be concerned that in the rush to stabilize Egypt, the Administration could be too lenient in terms of the reforms it seeks from the Egyptian government. Second, other lawmakers may not want the Administration to push for tough conditions on an IMF loan, fearing that onerous conditions could risk the Egyptian government avoiding an IMF loan and risking economic collapse, and/or risk pushing the Egyptian government to other sources of financing that may not be aligned with U.S. interests.

If Congress wants to influence U.S. policy toward Egypt at the IMF, it has legislative tools at its disposal to do so. The executive branch, through the Treasury Department, manages day-to-day participation of the United States in the IMF, but Congress over the years has passed a number of "legislative mandates" that impact actions of the U.S. Executive Director at the IMF. Often, but not exclusively, included in appropriations bills, legislative mandates can direct U.S. representatives at the IMF to advocate certain policies, direct the U.S. Executive Director to vote for or against certain types of programs or policies, and/or require the Treasury Department to submit reports to Congress on IMF issues or activities. Existing legislative mandates focused on specific countries direct the U.S. representatives at international financial institutions (IFIs) to, for example, oppose non-humanitarian assistance to a specific country (as in the case of Belarus[44]); advocate assistance to help a government improve its economic system and accelerate development (as in the case of Mongolia[45]); or oppose any non-humanitarian financial assistance to a specific country until certain political conditions have been met (as in the case of Zimbabwe[46]). Congress could pass similar legislation directing the "voice and vote" of the U.S. Executive Director at the IMF with regard to IMF programs and policies toward Egypt. It could also pass resolutions laying out congressional views on IMF engagement with Egypt.

Using the IMF as a Benchmark for U.S. Assistance to Egypt

Some lawmakers may seek to use the terms of IMF conditions as "financial benchmarks" for the provision of existing or any new bilateral economic aid to Egypt.[47] One potential concern, however, is how stringent the conditionality attached to the IMF program would be. According to Egyptian economist Ashraf Swelam, "[a]t a time when the economic situation in Egypt is going from bad to worse, every new draft of the reform program submitted to the IMF—in the endless rounds of negotiations dating all the way back to February 2011—has been a watered down version of its predecessor."[48]

U.S. debt relief has already been tied to an IMF program (see *text box* below), and legislation has been introduced in the 113th Congress to require an IMF agreement as a condition for U.S. bilateral assistance. Specifically, during Senate debate in March 2013 over the full-year continuing resolution (H.R. 933, passed into law as P.L. 113-6), a proposed amendment (S.Amdt. 44) would have, if adopted, conditioned the obligation of U.S. economic assistance to Egypt on the President's certification, among other things, that the Government of Egypt has "signed and submitted to the International Monetary Fund a Letter of Intent and Memorandum of Economic and Financial Policies designed to promote critical economic reforms and has begun to implement such measures." This amendment was not included in the final legislation as enacted.

U.S. Debt Relief for Egypt

On September 28, 2012, the Administration notified Congress of its intent to provide a $450 million cash transfer to Egypt (comprised of unobligated Economic Support Funds previously appropriated for other purposes) in order to repay its debts owed to or guaranteed by the United States. According to USAID, the $450 million was to be distributed in two tranches. The first tranche of $190 million would be released to the government of Egypt upon "the issuance of a public statement from the [Government of Egypt] GOE of its commitment to a national economic and fiscal stabilization,[49] recovery, and governance reform plan and to reach an agreement with the International Monetary Fund (IMF) on a loan package." The second tranche of $260 million would be distributed once the United States government determined that:

> The GOE has committed to and/or achieved actions on a homegrown economic and fiscal stabilization, recovery, and governance reform program that accords with international standards. The GOE would implement such a program in coordination with international financial institutions, including the IMF. The GOE could commit to and/or achieve such actions as reducing and streamlining energy subsidies; improving the government financial management; and increasing taxation revenues through a broadened tax base and reducing tax exemptions.

The Congressional Notification was issued weeks after an attack against U.S. diplomatic facilities in Libya in September 2012, which led to the death of Ambassador Christopher Stevens, and a protest outside the U.S. Embassy in Cairo in which a mob breached the Embassy walls and replaced the U.S. flag with a black one associated with Islamist extremist movements. Many lawmakers were angered by Morsi's failure to condemn the act immediately, apologize for the incident, and take more forceful police measures to protect the Embassy.

Upon receipt of the Congressional Notification, Representative Kay Granger, Chair of the House Appropriations Subcommittee on State and Foreign Operations, placed a "hold" on the $450 million cash transfer, stating that "This proposal comes to Congress at a point when the U.S. - Egypt relationship has never been under more scrutiny, and rightly so. I am not convinced of the urgent need for this assistance and I cannot support it at this time. As Chair of the Subcommittee, I have placed a hold on these funds."[50] Then-House Foreign Affairs Committee Chair Ileana RosLehtinen also placed a hold on the aid.

The hold remained in place until lawmakers lifted it on the first tranche of $190 million only. [51] The notification of the release of these funds was made by Secretary of State John Kerry during his March 2013 visit to Egypt, where he said that, "In light of Egypt's extreme needs and President Morsi's assurance that he plans to complete the IMF process, today I advised him the United States will now provide the first $190 million of our pledged $450 million in budget support funds." As of April 2013, the second tranche of $260 million in cash transfer remains on hold.

OUTLOOK

Financial assistance from neighboring countries may reduce the immediate fiscal pressures on Egypt, but it does not address deeper structural problems in Egypt's economy. If Egypt ultimately fails to reach an agreement with the IMF, it could signal a temporary setback for the Obama Administration, or it may be indicative of an oncoming period characterized by less U.S.- Egyptian cooperation on economic matters. In testimony before the House Appropriations Subcommittee on State, Foreign Operations, and Related Programs, Secretary of State Kerry questioned whether the United States should be doing more to influence Egypt, when he remarked that:

> I can't give you assurances about what this current [Morsi] administration is going to do, because I think they're still sorting through that. And the die is not cast yet. That was the purpose of my visit [to Egypt] and the purpose of the money which I am grateful to you for releasing. Qatar has put another $2 billion at the availability of Egypt just in the last week or so. Before that, they put about $4 billion or $5 billion. Libya has loaned them $2 billion in the last week or so. And the IMF is in negotiating for $4.8 billion. We promised $1 billion and until I took the 190 [$190 million] that you kindly helped us to be able to provide, we didn't provide them with a dime, not a dime. We gave them a promise and a year later, we've given them zero. Now, you know, you don't buy your interests and you don't buy your— that's not what foreign aid is about. But I'll tell you, if you're not helpful to people in their time of need, if

you're not there, part of the process, it's very, very difficult to have the kind of leverage to say, a diverse pluralistic politics is critical to us when they say, what's it matter to you? You don't really care. You're not helping us. The other guys are helping us. Thank you, we'll, you know, do what we want to do.[52]

On the other hand, though U.S. officials may not entirely embrace aid from non-IMF sources for Egypt such as Qatar, the Administration may feel that it must deal cautiously with Morsi's government so that the United States does not alienate friendly elements of the Egyptian opposition. Some policymakers may feel that non-IMF lending for Egypt may keep Egypt's financial situation in shaky, but workable order, and help to stave off a worst case scenario. However, it remains uncertain whether President Morsi's government can receive non-IMF stopgap lending indefinitely, and on what terms.

End Notes

[1] For example, see H.Res. 87; H.R. 276; H.R. 416; H.R. 939; H.R. 1039; H.R. 1302; S. 201; and S. 207.

[2] Unless otherwise noted, data in this report is from the IMF, World Economic Outlook, April 2013 or the World Bank, World Development Indicators, 2013.

[3] World Bank, "Egypt: Positive Results from Knowledge Sharing and Modest Lending," Independent Evaluation Group Assistance Evaluation, 2009.

[4] World Bank, "Most Improved in Doing Business 2008," http://www.doingbusiness.org/reforms /top-reformers-2008.

[5] IMF, "Arab Republic of Egypt: 2010 Article IV Consultation," April 2010.

[6] Average consumer prices, end of year.

[7] IMF, "Arab Countries in Transition: Economic Outlook and Key Challenges," Prepared for the Deauville Partnership Ministerial Meeting, October 12, 2012, http://www.imf.org/external/ region/mcd/deauville/note101212.pdf.

[8] Economist Intelligence Unit, "Country Report: Egypt," March 2013.

[9] IMF, International Financial Statistics, 2013.

[10] For more background on the IMF, see CRS Report R42019, International Monetary Fund: Background and Issues for Congress, by Martin A. Weiss.

[11] For information about the tentative agreement, see IMF, "IMF Reaches Staff Level Agreement with Egypt on a US$3 Billion Stand-By Arrangement," June 5, 2011.

[12] "Bread Riots or Bankruptcy: Egypt faces stark Economic Choices," Christian Science Monitor, April 3, 2013.

[13] According to one IMF official, "The IMF arrangement included a number of benchmarks, which consisted of measures that were already in the government's economic plan, none of them related to privatization or requiring changes to the subsidy regime during the period of

(the) IMF arrangement." See, "IMF says it is still ready to help Egypt," Agence France Presse, June 30, 2011.

[14] Open Source Center, "MB Statement On Current Domestic And Regional Affairs," Document ID# GMP20110709966104, London, Ikwanweb (in English), July 9, 2011.

[15] Abdel Latif Wahba and Mariam Fam, "Egypt Gets $1 Billion from Saudi Arabia, Minister Says," Bloomberg, May 10, 2012.

[16] IMF, "IMF Reaches Staff-Level Agreement with Egypt on a US$4.8 Billion Stand-By Arrangement," November 20, 2012.

[17] Economist Intelligence Unit (EIU), Egypt: Country Report, February 13, 2013.

[18] Arvind Subramanian, "Egypt's $4.8 Billion IMF Loan: Could it Affect Gaza?" Peterson Institute, Interviews on Current Topics, November 20, 2012.

[19] Ibid.

[20] Steven A. Cook, "Is Egypt Too Big to Fail?," "From the Potomac to the Euphrates" blog on Council on Foreign Relations website, February 7, 2013.

[21] Heba Saleh, "Egypt Rules out IMF Emergency Finance," Financial Times, March 12, 2013.

[22] Al-Masry Al-Youm, "Energy Subsidies will Disappear by 2016, Says Minister," Egypt Independent, February 26, 2013; "Egypt's President Morsi Unveils Raft of Tax, Subsidy Reforms," Ahram Online, February 25, 2013.

[23] (No text available for this end note.)

[24] Al-Masry Al-Youm, "Bakers Threaten Strike if Govt Doesn't Shelve Bread Subsidy Plan," Egypt Independent, February 25, 2013.

[25] "Egypt Under IMF Spotlight as Loan Talks Resume," Reuters, April 3, 2013.

[26] Rob Minto, "Egypt: Qatar Loan Puts IMF on Hold," Financial Times, April 10, 2013; "Egypt Gets US$2 Bn Loan from Libya," Al-Masry Al-Youm Online, April 13, 2013.

[27] Mohsin khan, "Qatar to the Rescue—Again!" Reuters, April 10, 2013.

[28] Alaa Shahine, "Egypt's IMF Loan Talks in Cairo End Without Agreement," Bloomberg, April 16, 2013.

[29] Asma Alsharif, "Egypt's Soaring Energy Bill to Exceed Previous Estimate," Reuters, 2013.

[30] Paul Taylor, "Egypt Seen Muddling Through Without IMF," Reuters, April 16, 2013.

[31] Senate Appropriations Subcommittee on State, Foreign Operations and Related Programs, Hearing on Fiscal Year 2014 State Department Budget, April 18, 2013.

[32] Arvind Subramanian, "The Egyptian Stabilization Experience: An Analytical Retrospective," IMF Working Paper Wp/97/105, September 1997.

[33] For example, see Alison Elizabeth Chase, "The Politics of Lending and Reform: The International Monetary Fund and the Nation of Egypt," Stanford Journal of International Law, vol. 42 (2006), pp. 193-236.

[34] Bretton Woods Project, "Rehash of Failed Policies for Arab States?" June 13, 2011.

[35] Chatham House, "The Role of International Loans and Capital in Egypt's Transition," MENA Programme: Egypt Dialogue Workshop Report, September 2011.

[36] Kienle, Eberhard, Democracy and Economic Reform in Egypt, I.B.Tauris, New York, NY, 2001, page 152.

[37] Stephen Kalin, "In Anti-IMF March, Austerity Fears and Economic Disillusion," Egypt Independent, November 11, 2012.

[38] Ahmed Feteha, "Egypt and the IMF: Hardly Revolutionary," Ahram Online (in English), February 3, 2013; "Egyptians Split over IMF Loan: Opinion Poll," Ahram Online (in English), October 3, 2012.

[39] For example, see Aya Batrawy, "IMF Leaves Egypt after Hearing from Opposition," Associated Press, April 16, 2013.

[40] "U.S. Supports IMF Loan for Egypt to Stabilize Economy," Reuters, April 24, 2013.

[41] "U.S. Support for the Egyptian People," Department of State, March 3, 2013.

[42] Robert Kagan and Michele Dunne, "Standing by as Egypt Unravels," Washington Post, February 22, 2013.

[43] Heba Saleh, "Egypt Rules out IMF Emergency Finance," Financial Times, March 12, 2013.

[44] 22 USC 5811 note; P.L. 109-480.

[45] S.Res. 192.

[46] 22 USC 2151; P.L. 111-117.

[47] Previous U.S. economic aid in the form of cash transfer had been tied to specific economic reforms undertaken by the government of Egypt and verified by the U.S. State Department and USAID.

[48] "Egypt's Moral Hazard,"by Guest Blogger Ashraf Swelam for Steven A. Cook, Council on Foreign Relations, March 5, 2013.

[49] In November 2012, the IMF noted that "The Egyptian authorities have developed a national program that seeks to promote economic recovery, address the country's fiscal and balance of payments deficits, and lay the foundation for rapid job creation and socially balanced growth in the medium term." See, IMF, "IMF Reaches Staff-Level Agreement with Egypt on a US$4.8 Billion Stand-By Arrangement," Press Release No. 12/446, November 20, 2012.

[50] "Granger Holds Cash Transfer to Egypt," Rep. Kay Granger Press Release, September 28, 2012.

[51] "Obama Push to Aid Egypt Remains Stalled in Congress," CQ Roll Call, November 13, 2012.

[52] House Appropriations Subcommittee on State, Foreign Operations, and Related Programs, Hearing on President Obama's Fiscal 2014 Budget Proposal for the State Department and Foreign Affairs, April 17, 2013.

INDEX

A

B

C

F

G

H

I